If, then, the tree may be known by
the fruit, as the fruit by the tree . . .

1 Henry IV, II, 4, 470–71

THE GRAFTON PORTRAIT

Reproduced by permission of the Director, The John Rylands Library, Manchester.

The young man shown here, of exactly Shakespeare's years, has not been identified. The painting was for long in the possession of the Ludgate family of Grafton Regis, Northamptonshire. An attempt has been made to trace its ownership to Shakespeare's granddaughter, Elizabeth Hall, who once lived nearby; cf. Keen and Lubbock, *The Annotator*, page 200.

THE CASE FOR
SHAKESPEARE'S
AUTHORSHIP

OF

The Famous Victories

With the complete text of the anonymous play

SEYMOUR M. PITCHER

Professor of English and General Literature
Harpur College, State University of New York

STATE UNIVERSITY OF NEW YORK

1961

Elmer Edgar Stoll (1874–1959)

IN MEMORIAM

ACKNOWLEDGMENTS

In the completion of this study I have particularly availed myself of the resources and services of the libraries of the State University of Iowa and Harpur College (State University of New York), of the New York State Library, of the New York Public Library, and of the Folger Shakespeare Library. The latter has permitted me to reproduce several important items. The Bodleian Library has authorized the reproduction of the title page of the 1598 edition of *The Famous Victories*. Professor Edward Robertson, Director of The John Rylands Library, has allowed the use of a photograph of the "Grafton Portrait." The Houghton Mifflin Company and The Macmillan Company have respectively sanctioned the use of, and quotation from, J. Q. Adams' edition of *The Famous Victories*, in *Chief Pre-Shakespearean Dramas* (1924, *et. seq.*) and Keen and Lubbock, *The Annotator* (1954). Foreign rights, in the case of the latter book, were waived by Putnam and Co., Ltd. The Macmillan Company has sanctioned the reprinting of a large number of marginal annotations in a copy of Hall's chronicle (1550), discussed at some length in Keen and Lubbock, *The Annotator* (1954). Mrs. Ruth Bellamy, production editor for University Publishers, and her assistant, Mrs. Olga Hoyt, have been most helpful in the preparation of the manuscript for the press. Also appreciated was the editorial assistance of Arnold Andersen.

I am much indebted to friends—particularly to Patrick Hamilton Ewing—who have made suggestions regarding the argument and its presentation. Finally, my thanks go to the Research Foundation of the State University of New York, which subsidized this undertaking, and to the Publications Committee of its Graduate Council, which authorized it.

S. M. P.

CONTENTS

ILLUSTRATIONS

THE CASE FOR

SHAKESPEARE'S AUTHORSHIP OF

The Famous Victories

PREFATORY REMARKS

Some years ago I became convinced that *The Famous Victories of Henry the Fifth* was written by William Shakespeare, and I have since tested the idea in a detailed study of the play and its background. Now I state my case.

I do not expect many to welcome with enthusiasm the opinion that this anonymous playlet, certainly dating from the period of Shakespeare's apprenticeship in the theater, is indeed his. Few will unhesitatingly embrace my innovation, for, they will rightly say, there is somewhat at stake, and much to be reconsidered. I anticipate that the more conservative among scholarly specialists, committed by predilection to familiar notions, will prefer to remain comfortable amidst uncertainties. Yet the canon of authentic works, established by Heming and Condell in 1623,[1] has

---

[1] Presumably Heming and Condell knew the authorship of *The Famous Victories,* for Heming may well have been a member of the company which enacted it; cf. Chambers (1923), II, 107. (For bibliography, see App. C, Books and Articles Used.) If Shakespeare wrote the play, the editors perhaps thought it otiose to include it with those it foreshadowed.

not proved inviolable. It is true that most of the so-called "apocryphal" plays have been repudiated,[2] but *Pericles, Prince of Tyre,* and *The Two Noble Kinsmen* have come to be widely accepted as being for the most part genuine, together with the "D" revisions of *Sir Thomas More.* Further additions may perhaps occur.

The Famous Victories, in span of events, approximates the familiar trilogy dealing with Henry of Monmouth; in length, it is but half one of them. Omitting the civil strife of the reign of Henry IV and beginning with the robbery at Gad's Hill, it emphasizes the wildness of the young Prince Henry in several episodes, brings him to reconciliation with his father, shows him after his coronation dismissing his rascally companions and proclaiming his expedition to France, then provides his final triumph at Agincourt and with the Lady Katherine. Being unpretentious and inferior, the play has escaped steady scrutiny.[3] Most often, since Theobald (in 1733) indicated his "suspicion," it has been tagged as a source for the greater three,[4] but there has been uneasiness among those who have probed the matter. Thus John Dover Wilson, jeopardizing his own conclusions, admits dissatisfaction: "Without any doubt whatever a very intimate connexion of some kind exists between Shakespeare's three plays and this old text, though what the connexion is has never been established."[5] This statement licenses further speculation.

-----

[2] The subject has recently been reviewed by Maxwell, *passim.*

[3] There have been various editions and a number of monographs on the subject; see App. C, and cf. Chambers (1923), IV, 17. In this country the play is available only in Adams' anthology.

[4] Cf. Hemingway, p. 448.

[5] Wilson (1945), p. 3. For his conclusions, see pp. 163–65.

The Famous Victories is, in any case, worth investigation. True, it has been frequently reprobated both as text and as play, but in its own time it must have had considerable effect. "What a glorious thing it is," said Thomas Nash in 1592, referring presumably to its last scene, "to have Henry the Fifth represented on the stage, leading the French King prisoner and forcing him and the Dolphin to swear fealty!" [6] Comment since then has usually been less appreciative,[7] though John Addington Symonds observes "the artless and sturdy straightforwardness of the stage-carpenter of plays who made it," and proclaims it "a piece of uncouth but honest old English upholstery." [8] Of poetry quite devoid, it yet manifests, I think, extraordinary power of expression and a sense of human realities. It is not at all unworthy of Shakespeare as a spirited and genial apprentice dramatist. Moreover, since, as will presently be shown, 1586 is the most likely date of its composition, it may be his first play, at twenty-two.

We do not, of course, know much about Shakespeare's

---

[6] Nash, I, 213, in *Pierce Penniless;* see pp. 179–80. What seem to be echoes of the play's title are long heard; see Explanatory Notes: TITLE.

[7] A. F. Hopkinson, p. xii, summarizes opinion at the end of the nineteenth century: "Certain critics have alluded to this play in terms of unqualified disparagement. Capell wrote of it as 'a medley of nonsense and ribaldry,' a 'miserable performance,' and marked 'its fate, which was damnation'; Dyce calls it a 'worthless play,' and Mr. Halliwell-Phillips applies to it the epithet 'contemptible.' . . . This censure seems to me too severe . . . considering the early date at which it was written, there is much in it superior to anything that had appeared prior to its production." More recent criticism has continued unfriendly; thus Harrison, pp. 614–15, calls it "a crude piece," "poor low comedy," "primitive"; and F. P. Wilson, p. 106, finds it "a play of incredible meanness in the form in which it has come down to us."

[8] Symonds, p. 378.

literary beginnings. None of the highly competent "early" plays of the canon can be described as inexperienced writing. *The Famous Victories* is a clatter of events, its quick narrative interspersed with light and raucous comedy. Comical-historical it surely is, but in its hybrid form sufficiently self-consistent in tone. Sketchy and sometimes banal, it is gusty and flaunting. At best, it has poignancy in characterization and phrase. How else should we expect Shakespeare to have begun?

It seems impossible that the play was his mere source for the later three. He used it ingeniously, as he used his sources, but more than that, he used it instinctively as if it were his own. He knew it by heart, by total assimilation. Presumably not a first draft by intention, it served him as such, and by the tedious—and devious—ways of art, it at last evolved into the trilogy. A source, to be sure, may offer a second writer fresh motivation, stores for plunder, materials to cast anew, but in contrast a first draft grows, sometimes with abrupt mutations here and there, from what it has been to what it can, and perhaps must, become; the development that it undergoes is largely internal and organic. And it was thus, I believe, that *The Famous Victories* became the ultimate trilogy,[9] exercising an imperious control over the later characterizations of Hal as princeling and king, of his father, and of Sir John Falstaff. For a decade, more or less, it was dynamic in Shakespeare's stockpile of stuff.

---

[9] Daniel, p. iii, also makes this point: "It offers us what seems to be the germ of the brilliant comedy with which Shakespeare enriched the history; and accordingly in this poor play [*sic*] we follow the fortunes of the royal hero and the 'irregular humorists' his companions . . . with something of the interest a biologist may be supposed to feel in tracing the progress of some low organism to its latest development as a perfect creature." Cf. Goddard, pp. 17–19.

The bookish but still gentle and unjaded reader will no doubt agree that it would be an enterprise of pith to establish Shakespeare's authorship of any play not previously known as his. It is not easy to explain why those who have sought traces of his earliest activity have overlooked *The Famous Victories*.[10] To demonstrate the play to be his would not only enlarge and clarify our conceptions of his youthful powers and mentality; we should have taken a step toward dissipating the mystery of the "dark" years of his life. We should then know that he came to London no ignorant bumpkin. He cannot long have held horses at theater doors or been prompter's assistant, as some traditions have it.[11] This immature play, despite its slapstick and buffoonery, would prove him early read. Its author had spent hours with "rusty brass and worm-eaten books,"[12] piecing his story from the chronicle histories of Edward Hall, Raphael Holinshed, and John Stow. Influential in determining his conception of young Prince Henry was an anecdote told by Sir Thomas Elyot in *The Book of the Governor*.

We should have established the probability that Shakespeare began his career as a playwright. We should know that, as of 1586, it was in this capacity that he was in the

---

[10] Everitt alone approaches my thesis, cautiously suggesting (p. 171) that "we keep in mind" the chance of Shakespearean authorship. Various other attributions have been made unsuccessfully. Ward (1928, *R.E.S.*), p. 294, proposed the Earl of Oxford. This claim he does not sustain in his biography; cf. p. 336, note. Fleay (1891), II, 259, nominated Richard Tarlton; and Greg (1922), pp. 360–61, suggests that Tarlton may have written the part of Derick for himself. Sykes offers Samuel Rowley, but is criticized by Greg, *loc. cit.*

[11] Recorded by Johnson and Malone; cf. Halliwell-Phillips (1857), I, 80–84.

[12] Nash, I, 212, uses this phrase.

employ of the Queen's Players, the chief acting company of the decade. *The Famous Victories* belonged to their repertory. Richard Tarlton, the most popular comedian of his own—and perhaps any—day, quickened the role of Derick the Clown when the play was staged at the Bull Inn at Bishopsgate with William Knell playing Henry V. Presumably the piece was shown before the Queen at about the same time, and it may later have toured the provinces, with a stand at Stratford.[13]

In the following argument I assume in the reader some knowledge of Shakespeare's *1* and *2 Henry IV* and *Henry V*. The most important witness is the old play itself. Since it is not readily available, I present it herewith. I have taken advantage of the work of J. Q. Adams, who printed the piece as the prose it is, and who made many improvements upon the received texts.[14] In my edition, punctuation and capitalization have been altered, spelling has been modernized, stage directions have been amplified (*additions in brackets*), explanatory notes elaborated. The argument for Shakespearean authorship is set forth under various heads, and the play's source materials are included in an appendix.

---

[13] See pp. 173, 182.
[14] See Explanatory Notes, following text of the play, pp. 70–79, *passim*.

TEXT OF

The Famous Victories
of Henry the Fifth

[DRAMATIS PERSONAE

KING HENRY THE FOURTH
PRINCE HENRY OF MONMOUTH, *his son*
    (*later* KING HENRY THE FIFTH)
DUKE OF YORK ⎫
DUKE OF EXETER ⎬ *brothers of Henry IV*
EARL OF OXFORD
ARCHBISHOP OF CANTERBURY
THE LORD CHIEF JUSTICE
THE LORD MAYOR OF LONDON
THE SHERIFF
NED ⎫
TOM ⎬ *Knights*
SIR JOHN OLDCASTLE, *alias* JOCKEY ⎭
ENGLISH CAPTAIN
ENGLISH SOLDIER
TWO RECEIVERS
CLERK OF THE KING'S BENCH
THE JAILER
THE THIEF, CUTBERT CUTTER, *alias* "GAD'S HILL"
DERICK, *a poor carrier*
JOHN COBBLER ⎫
ROBIN PEWTERER ⎬ *the Watch*
LAWRENCE COSTERMONGER ⎭
THE VINTNER'S BOY, ROBIN
THE PORTER
KING CHARLES VI, *of France*
THE DOLPHIN, *his son*
DUKE OF BURGUNDY
ARCHBISHOP OF BOURGES
THE CONSTABLE
A HERALD
A MESSENGER
A FRENCH CAPTAIN
JACK DRUMMER
THREE FRENCH SOLDIERS
A FRENCHMAN

PRINCESS KATHERINE, *daughter of Charles VI*
MISTRESS COBBLER

LORDS, LADIES, ATTENDANTS

        SCENE—*England and France*]

THE FAMOUS VICTORIES

Of Henry the Fifth

Containing the
Honorable Battle of Agincourt.

[SCENE ONE.]

[A mile off London. Eve of St. John Baptist, 1410.]

Enter the young PRINCE, NED, *and* TOM.

Prince. Come away, Ned and Tom.

Both. Here, my lord.

Prince. Come away, my lads. Tell me, sirs, how much gold have you got?

Ned. Faith, my lord, I have got five hundred pound.   5

Prince. But tell me, Tom, how much hast thou got?

Tom. Faith, my lord, some four hundred pound.

Prince. Four hundred pounds! Bravely spoken, lads! But tell me, sirs, think you not that it was a villainous part of me to rob my father's receivers?   10

Ned. Why, no, my lord; it was but a trick of youth.

Prince. Faith, Ned, thou sayest true. But tell me, sirs, whereabouts are we?

Tom. My lord, we are now about a mile off London.

Prince. But, sirs, I marvel that Sir John Oldcastle comes   15
not away. Zounds! see where he comes.

Enter JOCKEY.

How now, Jockey, what news with thee?

Jockey. Faith, my lord, such news as passeth! For the
town of Deptford is risen with hue and cry after your man,
which parted from us the last night and has set upon and   20
hath robbed a poor carrier.

Prince. Zounds! the villain that was wont to spy out our
booties?

Jockey. Ay, my lord, even the very same.

Prince. Now base-minded rascal to rob a poor carrier!   25
Well, it skills not; I'll save the base villain's life, if I may.
But tell me, Jockey, whereabouts be the receivers?

Jockey. Faith, my lord, they are hard by; but the best is
we are ahorseback and they be afoot, so we may escape
them.   30

Prince. Well, if the villains come, let me alone with them!
But tell me, Jockey, how much gotst thou from the knaves?
For I am sure I got something, for one of the villains so be-
lamed me about the shoulders as I shall feel it this month.

Jockey. Faith, my lord, I have got a hundred pound.   35

Prince. A hundred pound! Now bravely spoken, Jockey.
But come, sirs, lay all your money before me. Now, by
heaven, here is a brave show! But, as I am a true gentleman,
I will have the half of this spent to-night! But, sirs, take up
your bags; here come the receivers. Let me alone   40

Enter two RECEIVERS.

First Receiver. Alas, good fellow, what shall we do? I
dare never go home to the Court, for I shall be hanged. But
look, here is the young Prince. What shall we do?

Prince. How now, you villains! What are you?

First Receiver. Speak you to him. 45

Second Receiver. No, I pray, speak you to him.

Prince. Why, how now, you rascals! Why speak you not?

First Receiver. Forsooth, we be—pray speak you to him.

Prince. Zounds, villains, speak, or I'll cut off your heads! 50

Second Receiver. Forsooth, he can tell the tale better than I.

First Receiver. Forsooth, we be your father's receivers.

Prince. Are you my father's receivers? Then I hope you have brought me some money. 55

First Receiver. Money? Alas, sir, we be robbed!

Prince. Robbed! How many were there of them?

First Receiver. Marry, sir, there were four of them; and one of them had Sir John Oldcastle's bay hobby, and your black nag. 60

Prince. Gog's wounds! How like you this, Jockey? Blood, you villains! my father robbed of his money abroad, and we robbed in our stables! But tell me, how many were of them?

First Receiver. If it please you, there were four of them; and there was one about the bigness of you:—but I am sure I 65 so belamed him about the shoulders that he will feel it this month.

Prince. Gog's wounds! You lamed them fairly—so that they have carried away your money. But come, sirs, what shall we do with the villains? 70

Both Receivers. I beseech your Grace, be good to us.

Ned. I pray you, forgive them this once.

Prince. Well, stand up, and get you gone. And look that you speak not a word of it—for, if there be—zounds! I'll hang you and all your kin! 75

[*Exeunt* RECEIVERS.]

Prince. Now, sirs, how like you this? Was not this bravely done? For now the villains dare not speak a word of it, I have so feared them with words. Now, whither shall we go?

All. Why, my lord, you know our old host's at Favers-   80
ham.

Prince. Our host's at Faversham! Blood, what shall we do there? We have a thousand pound about us, and we shall go to a petty ale-house? No, no! You know the old tavern in Eastcheap; there is good wine:—besides, there is a pretty wench that can talk well; for I delight as much in their   85
tongues as any part about them.

All. We are ready to wait upon your Grace.

Prince. Gog's wounds! "Wait"? We will go altogether; we are all fellows. I tell you, sirs, if the King my father were dead, we would be all kings. Therefore, come away!   90

Ned. Gog's wounds, bravely spoken, Harry!

[*Exeunt omnes.*]

[SCENE TWO.]

[*Billingsgate Ward, London.*]

Enter JOHN COBBLER, ROBIN PEWTERER,
LAWRENCE COSTERMONGER.

John. All is well here; all is well, masters.

Lawrence. How say you, neighbor John Cobbler? I think it best that my neighbor, Robin Pewterer, went to Pudding Lane End, and we will watch here at Billings-gate Ward. How say you, neighbor Robin? how like you   5
this?

Robin. Marry, well, neighbors; I care not much if I go to Pudding Lane's End. But, neighbors, if you hear any ado

about me, make haste; and if I hear any ado about you, I will
come to you. 10

Exit ROBIN.

Lawrence. Neighbor, what news hear you of the young
Prince?

John. Marry, neighbor, I hear say he is a toward young
Prince; for, if he meet any by the highway, he will not let
to—talk with him. I dare not call him thief, but sure he is one 15
of these taking fellows.

Lawrence. Indeed, neighbor, I hear say he is as lively a
young Prince as ever was.

John. Ay, and I hear say if he use it long, his father will
cut him off from the crown. But, neighbor, say nothing of 20
that!

Lawrence. No, no neighbor, I warrant you!

John. Neighbor, methinks you begin to sleep. If you will,
we will sit down; for I think it is about midnight.

Lawrence. Marry, content, neighbor; let us sleep. 25

Enter DERICK, *roving.*

Derick. Whoa! whoa, there! whoa, there!

Exit DERICK. *Enter* ROBIN.

Robin. Oh, neighbors, what mean you to sleep, and such
ado in the streets?

Both. How now, neighbor, what's the matter?

Enter DERICK *again.*

Derick. Whoa, there! whoa, there! whoa, there! 30
John. Why, what ailst thou? here is no horses.

Derick. O alas, man, I am robbed! whoa there! whoa there!

Robin. Hold him, neighbor Cobbler. [*He pinions* DER-ICK.] Why, I see thou art a plain clown.   35

DERICK. Am I a clown? Zounds, masters, do clowns go in silk apparel? I am sure all we gentlemen-clowns in Kent scant go so well. Zounds! you know clowns very well! Hear you, are you Master Constable? If you be, speak, for I will not take it at his hands.   40

John. Faith, I am not Master Constable; but I am one of his bad officers, for he is not here.

Derick. Is not Master Constable here? Well, it is no matter. I'll have the law at his hands.

John. Nay, I pray you, do not take the law of us.   45

Derick. Well, you are one of his beastly officers.

John. I am one of his bad officers.

Derick. Why, then, I charge thee, look to him!

John. Nay, but hear you, sir; you seem to be an honest fellow, and we are poor men; and now 'tis night, and we   50
would be loath to have anything ado; therefore, I pray thee, put it up. [*Indicating* DERICK's *dagger.*]

Derick. First, thou sayest true; I am an honest fellow— and a proper, handsome fellow, too! and you seem to be poor men; therefore I care not greatly. Nay, I am quickly   55
pacified. But, if you chance to spy out the thief, I pray you lay hold on him.

Robin. Yes, that we will, I warrant you. [*He releases* DERICK.]

Derick. [*Aside.*] 'Tis a wonderful thing to see how glad   60
the knave is, now I have forgiven him.

John. Neighbors, do you look about you. How now, who's there?

Enter the THIEF.

Thief. Here is a good fellow. I pray you, which is the
way to the old tavern in Eastcheap? 65

Derick. Whoop halloo! Now, "Gad's Hill," knowest
thou me?

Thief. I know thee for an ass.

Derick. And I know thee for a taking fellow upon Gad's
Hill in Kent. A bots light upon you! 70

Thief. The whoreson villain would be knocked.

Derick. Villain! Masters, if you be men, stand to him,
and take his weapon from him. Let him not pass you!

John. My friend, what make you abroad now? It is too
late to walk now. 75

Thief. It is not too late for true men to walk.

Lawrence. We know thee not to be a true man.

[*They seize the* THIEF.]

Thief. Why, what do you mean to do with me? Zounds!
I am one of the King's liege people.

Derick. Hear you, sir, are you one of the King's liege 80
people?

Thief. Ay, marry am I, sir! What say you to it?

Derick. Marry, sir, I say you are one of the King's filching people.

John. Come, come, let's have him away. 85

Thief. Why, what have I done?

Robin. Thou hast robbed a poor fellow, and taken away
his goods from him.

Thief. I never saw him before.

Derick. Masters, who comes here? 90

Enter the VINTNER'S BOY.

Boy. How now, goodman Cobbler.

John. How now, Robin, what makest thou abroad at this time of night?

Boy. Marry, I have been at the Counter; I can tell such news as never you have heard the like!   95

John. What is that, Robin? What is the matter?

Boy. Why, this night, about two hours ago, there came the young Prince, and three or four more of his companions, and called for wine good store; and then they sent for a noise of musicians, and were very merry for the space of an hour;   100 then, whether their music liked them not, or whether they had drunk too much wine or no, I cannot tell, but our pots flew against the walls; and then they drew their swords and went into the street and fought, and some took one part and some took another; but for the space of half an hour there   105 was such a bloody fray as passeth! And none could part them until such time as the Mayor and Sheriff were sent for; and then, at the last, with much ado, they took them; and so the young Prince was carried to the Counter; and then, about one hour after, there came a messenger from   110 the Court in all haste from the King for my Lord Mayor and the Sheriff—but for what cause I know not.

John. Here is news, indeed, Robert!

Lawrence. Marry, neighbor, this news is strange, indeed! I think it best, neighbor, to rid our hands of this fellow first.   115

Thief. What mean you to do with me?

John. We mean to carry you to the prison, and there to remain till the sessions day.

Thief. Then, I pray you, let me go to the prison where my master is.   120

John. Nay, thou must go to the country prison, to New-gate. Therefore, come away.

Thief. [*To* DERICK.] I prithee, be good to me, honest fellow.

Derick. Ay, marry, will I; I'll be very charitable to thee,   125
for I will never leave thee—till I see thee on the gallows.

[*Exeunt omnes.*]

[Scene Three.]

[*Westminster Palace.*]

Enter Henry the Fourth [*attended*],
with the Earl of Exeter, *and the* Lord of Oxford.

Oxford. If [it] please your Majesty, here is my Lord
Mayor and the Sheriff of London to speak with your
Majesty.

King. Admit them to our presence.

Enter the Mayor *and the* Sheriff.

King. Now, my good Lord Mayor of London, the cause   5
of my sending for you at this time is to tell you of a matter
which I have learned of my Council. Herein I understand
that you have committed my son to prison without our leave
and license. What! although he be a rude youth, and likely
to give occasion, yet you might have considered that he is a   10
Prince, and my son, and not to be haled to prison by every
subject.

Mayor. May it please your Majesty to give us leave to tell
our tale?

King. Or else God forbid! Otherwise, you might think   15
me an unequal judge, having more affection to my son than
to any rightful judgement.

Mayor. Then I do not doubt but we shall rather deserve
commendations at your Majesty's hands than any anger.

King. Go to, say on.   20

Mayor. Then, if it please your Majesty, this night betwixt two and three of the clock in the morning my lord the
young Prince, with a very disordered company, came to the
old tavern in Eastcheap; and whether it was that their music
liked them not, or whether they were overcome with wine,   25
I know not, but they drew their swords, and into the street
they went; and some took my lord the young Prince's part,
and some took the other; but betwixt them there was such a
bloody fray for the space of half an hour that neither watchmen nor any other could stay them; till my brother, the   30
Sheriff of London, and I were sent for; and, at the last, with
much ado, we stayed them. But it was long first, which was
a great disquieting to all your loving subjects thereabouts.
And then, my good lord, we knew not whether your Grace
had sent them to try us whether we would do justice, or   35
whether it were of their own voluntary will or not, we cannot tell. And, therefore, in such a case, we knew not what to
do; but, for our own safeguard, we sent him to ward; where
he wanteth nothing that is fit for his Grace and your
Majesty's son. And thus, most humbly beseeching your   40
Majesty to think of our answer—

King. Stand aside until we have further deliberated on
your answer.

Exeunt MAYOR [*and* SHERIFF].

King. Ah, Harry! Harry! now thrice-accursed Harry,
that hath gotten a son which with grief will end his father's   45
days! Oh, my son, a prince thou art, ay, a prince indeed—
and to deserve imprisonment! And well have they done, and
like faithful subjects. [*To his* ATTENDANTS.] Discharge
them, and let them go.

Exeter. I beseech your Grace, be good to my lord the   50
young Prince.

King. Nay, nay, 'tis no matter; let him alone.

Oxford. Perchance the Mayor and the Sheriff have been too precise in this matter.

King. No, they have done like faithful subjects. I will go   55
myself to discharge them and let them go.

[*Exeunt omnes.*]

[SCENE FOUR.]

[*The Court of the King's Bench.*]

Enter the LORD CHIEF JUSTICE, *the* CLERK OF THE OFFICE,
   the JAILER, JOHN COBBLER, DERICK, *and the* THIEF.

Judge. Jailer, bring the prisoner to the bar.

Derick. Hear you, my lord; I pray you, bring the bar to the prisoner.

Judge. Hold thy hand up at the bar.

Thief. Here it is, my lord.   5

Judge. Clerk of the Office, read his indictment.

Clerk. What is thy name?

Thief. My name was known before I came here, and shall be when I am gone, I warrant you.

Judge. Ay, I think so; but we will know it better before   10
thou go.

Derick. Zounds! if you do but send to the next jail, we are sure to know his name; for this is not the first prison he hath been in, I'll warrant you.

Clerk. What is thy name?   15

Thief. What need you ask, and have it in writing?

Clerk. Is not thy name Cutbert Cutter?

Thief. What the devil need you ask, and know it so well?

Clerk. Why then, Cutbert Cutter, I indict thee, by the 20
name of Cutbert Cutter, for robbing a poor carrier the 20th
day of May last past, in the fourteenth year of the reign of
our sovereign lord King Henry the Fourth, for setting upon
a poor carrier upon Gad's Hill, in Kent, and having beaten
and wounded the said carrier, and taken his goods from 25
him—

Derick. Oh, masters, stay there! Nay, let's never belie the
man! for he hath not [only] beaten and wounded me also,
but he hath beaten and wounded my pack, and hath taken
the great raze of ginger that Bouncing Bess with the jolly 30
buttocks should have had. That grieves me most.

Judge. Well, what sayest thou? Art thou guilty, or not
guilty?

Thief. Not guilty, my lord.

Judge. By whom wilt thou be tried? 35

Thief. By my lord the young Prince, or by myself,
whether you will.

Enter the young PRINCE, *with* NED *and* TOM.

Prince. Come away, my lads. Gog's wounds, you villain!
what make you here? I must go about my business myself
and you must stand loitering here? 40

Thief. Why, my lord, they have bound me, and will not
let me go.

Prince. Have they bound thee, villain? Why, how now,
my lord?

Judge. I am glad to see your Grace in good health. 45

Prince. Why, my lord, this is my man. 'Tis marvel you
knew him not long before this. I tell you, he is a man of his
hands.

Thief. Ay, Gog's wounds, that I am! Try me, who dare.
[*He postures.*] 50

Judge. Your Grace shall find small credit by acknowledging him to be your man.

Prince. Why, my lord, what hath he done?

Judge. If it please your Majesty, he hath robbed a poor carrier.   55

Derick. Hear you, sir; marry, it was one Derick, goodman Hobling's man, of Kent.

Prince. What! was't you, buttonbreech? Of my word, my lord, he did it but in jest.

Derick. Hear you, sir, is it your man's quality to rob folks   60
in jest? In faith, he shall be hanged in earnest.

Prince. Well, my lord, what do you mean to do with my man?

Judge. If [it] please your Grace, the law must pass on him according to justice; then he must be executed.   65

Prince. Why, then, belike you mean to hang my man?

Judge. I am sorry that it falls out so.

Prince. Why, my lord, I pray you, who am I?

Judge. If it please your Grace, you are my lord the young Prince, our king that shall be after the decease of our   70
sovereign lord King Henry the Fourth, whom God grant long to reign!

Prince. You say true, my lord. And you will hang my man?

Judge. If it like your Grace, I must needs do justice.   75

Prince. Tell me, my lord, shall I have my man?

Judge. I cannot, my lord.

Prince. But will you not let him go?

Judge. I am sorry that his case is so ill.

Prince. Tush! case me no casings! Shall I have my man?   80

Judge. I cannot, nor I may not, my lord.

Prince. Nay, and "I shall not," say—and then I am answered?

Judge. No.
Prince. No! Then I will have him.   85

He gives him a box on the ear.

Ned. Gog's wounds, my lord, shall I cut off his head?
Prince. No. I charge you, draw not your swords. But get
you hence. Provide a noise of musicians. Away, be gone!

Exeunt NED *and* TOM.

Judge. Well, my lord, I am content to take it at your
hands.   90
Prince. Nay, if you be not, you shall have more!
Judge. Why, I pray you, my lord, who am I?
Prince. You! who knows not you? Why, man, you are
Lord Chief Justice of England.
Judge. Your Grace hath said truth; therefore, in striking   95
me in this place you greatly abuse me; and not me only but
also your father, whose lively person here in this place I do
represent. And therefore to teach you what prerogatives
mean, I commit you to the Fleet until we have spoken with
your father.   100
Prince. Why, then, belike you mean to send me to the
Fleet!
Judge. Ay, indeed; and therefore, carry him away.

[*Exit* PRINCE *with the* OFFICERS.]

Judge. Jailer, carry the prisoner to Newgate until the
next assizes.   105
Jailer. At your commandment, my lord, it shall be
done.

[*Exeunt all except* DERICK *and* JOHN COBBLER.]

Derick. [*Aside.*] Zounds, masters, here's ado when princes
must go to prison! Why, John, didst ever see the like?

John. O Derick, trust me, I never saw the like!   110

Derick. Why, John, thou mayst see what princes be in
choler. A judge a box on the ear! I'll tell thee, John, O John,
I would not have done it for twenty shillings.

John. No, nor I. There had been no way but one with us
—we should have been hanged.   115

Derick. Faith, John, I'll tell thee what; thou shalt be my
Lord Chief Justice, and thou shalt sit in the chair; and I'll be
the young prince, and hit thee a box on the ear; and then
thou shalt say, "To teach you what prerogatives mean, I
commit you to the Fleet."   120

John. Come on; I'll be your judge! But thou shalt not hit
me hard?

Derick. No, no.

[John Cobbler *takes the* Judge's *seat.*]

John. What hath he done?

Derick. Marry, he hath robbed Derick.   125

John. Why, then, I cannot let him go.

Derick. I must needs have my man.

John. You shall not have him!

Derick. Shall I not have my man? Say No, if you dare!
How say you? Shall I not have my man?   130

John. No, marry, shall you not!

Derick. Shall I not, John?

John. No, Derick.

Derick. Why, then, take you that [*boxing his ear*] till
more come! Zounds, shall I not have him?   135

John. Well, I am content to take this at your hand. But,
I pray you, who am I?

Derick. Who art thou? Zounds, dost not know thyself?

John. No.

Derick. Now away, simple fellow. Why, man, thou art   140
John the Cobbler.

John. No, I am my Lord Chief Justice of England.

Derick. Oh, John, mass! thou sayst true, thou art indeed.

John. Why, then, to teach you what prerogatives mean,
I commit you to the Fleet.   145

Derick. Well, I will go; but, i'faith, you gray-beard
knave, I'll course you.

Exit. And straight enters again.

Derick. Oh, John, come, come out of thy chair. Why,
what a clown wert thou to let me hit thee a box on the ear!
And now thou seest they will not take me to the Fleet.   150
I think that thou art one of these Worenday clowns.

John. But I marvel what will become of thee.

Derick. Faith, I'll be no more a carrier.

John. What wilt thou do, then?

Derick. I'll dwell with thee, and be a cobbler.   155

John. With me? Alas, I am not able to keep thee. Why,
thou wilt eat me out of doors.

Derick. Oh, John! No, John; I am none of these great
slouching fellows that devour these great pieces of beef and
brews. Alas, a trifle serves me—a woodcock, a chicken, a   160
capon's leg, or any such little thing serves me.

John. A capon! Why, man, I cannot get a capon once a
year—except it be at Christmas, at some other man's house;
for we cobblers be glad of a dish of roots.

Derick. Roots! why, are you so good at rooting? Nay,   165
cobbler, we'll have you ringed.

John. But, Derick,

Though we be so poor,
Yet will we have in store
A crab in the fire,
With nut-brown ale
That is full stale,
Which will a man quail
And lay in the mire.

Derick. A bots on you! if [it] be but for your ale, I'll 175
dwell with you. Come, let's away as fast as we can.

Exeunt.

[Scene Five.]

[*Outside and within Westminster Palace.*]

Enter the young Prince, *with* Ned *and* Tom.

Prince. Come away, sirs. Gog's wounds, Ned! didst thou
not see what a box on the ear I took my Lord Chief
Justice?

Tom. By Gog's blood, it did me good to see it. It made his
teeth jar in his head!   5

Enter Sir John Oldcastle.

Prince. How now, Sir John Oldcastle, what news with
you?

John Oldcastle. I am glad to see your Grace at liberty. I
was come, I, to visit you in prison.

Prince. To visit me! Didst thou not know that I am a   10
prince's son? Why, 'tis enough for me to look into a prison,
though I come not in myself. But here's such ado nowadays
—here's prisoning, here's hanging, whipping, and the devil

and all. But I tell you, sirs, when I am King we will have no
such things. But, my lads, if the old King, my father, were   15
dead, we would be all kings.

John Oldcastle. He is a good old man; God take him to
his mercy the sooner!

Prince. But, Ned, so soon as I am King, the first thing I
will do shall be to put my Lord Chief Justice out of office,   20
and thou shalt be my Lord Chief Justice of England.

Ned. Shall I be Lord Chief Justice? By Gog's wounds,
I'll be the bravest Lord Chief Justice that ever was in England!

Prince. Then, Ned, I'll turn all these prisons into fence-   25
schools, and I will endue thee with them, with lands to maintain them withal. Then I will have a bout with my Lord
Chief Justice. Thou shalt hang none but pick-purses, and
horse-stealers, and such base-minded villains; but that fellow
that will stand by the highway side courageously with his   30
sword and buckler and take a purse—that fellow, give him
my commendations! Beside that, send him to me, and I will
give him an annual pension out of my exchequer to maintain him all the days of his life.

John. Nobly spoken, Harry! We shall never have a   35
merry world till the old king be dead.

Ned. But whither are you going now?

Prince. To the Court; for I hear say my father lies very
sick.

Tom. But I doubt he will not die.   40

Prince. Yet will I go thither; for the breath shall be no
sooner out of his mouth but I will clap the crown on my
head.

Jockey. [*John.*] Will you go to the Court with that cloak
so full of needles?   45

Prince. Cloak, eyelet-holes, needles, and all was of mine own devising; and therefore I will wear it.

Tom. I pray you, my lord, what may be the meaning thereof?

Prince. Why, man, 'tis a sign that I stand upon thorns till   50
the crown be on my head.

Jockey. Or that every needle might be a prick to their hearts that repine at your doings?

Prince. Thou sayst true, Jockey. But there's some will say the young Prince will be "a well toward young man"—   55
and all this gear, that I had as leave they would break my head with a pot as to say any such thing. But we stand prating here too long; I must needs speak with my father. Therefore, come away!

[*They go to the gate.*]

Porter. What a rapping keep you at the King's court-   60
gate?

Prince. Here's one that must speak with the King.

Porter. The King is very sick, and none must speak with him.

Prince. No? You rascal, do you not know me?   65

Porter. You are my lord the young Prince.

Prince. Then go and tell my father that I must, and will, speak with him.

Ned. Shall I cut off his head?

Prince. No, no. Though I would help you in other places,   70
yet I have nothing to do here. What! you are in my father's Court.

Ned. [*Aside.*] I will write him in my tables; for so soon as I am made Lord Chief Justice I will put him out of his office.   75

The trumpet sounds.

Prince. Gog's wounds, sirs, the King comes. Let's all stand aside.

Enter the KING, *with the* LORD OF EXETER.

King. And is it true, my lord, that my son is already sent to the Fleet? Now, truly, that man is more fitter to rule the realm than I; for by no means could I rule my son, and he, 80 by one word, hath caused him to be ruled. Oh, my son! my son! no sooner out of one prison but into another? I had thought once-whiles I had lived to have seen this noble realm of England flourish by thee, my son; but now I see it goes to ruin and decay. 85

He weeps.

Enter LORD OF OXFORD.

Oxford. If [it] please your Grace, here is my lord your son that cometh to speak with you. He saith he must, and will, speak with you.

King. Who? My son Harry?

Oxford. Ay, if [it] please your Majesty. 90

King. I know wherefore he cometh. But look that none come with him.

Oxford. A very disordered company, and such as make very ill rule in your Majesty's house.

King. Well, let him come; but look that none come with 95 him.

He goes.

Oxford. If [it] please your Grace, my lord the King sends for you.

Prince. Come away, sirs, let's go all together.

Oxford. If [it] please your Grace, none must go with 100 you.

Prince. Why, I must needs have them with me; otherwise
I can do my father no countenance: therefore, come away.

Oxford. The King your father commands there should
none come.   105

Prince. Well, sirs, then be gone—and provide me three
noise of musicians.

Exeunt KNIGHTS.

[SCENE SIX.]

[*A Secret Chamber, Westminster Palace.*]

Enter the PRINCE, *with a dagger in his hand,*
[*to the King, attended*].

King. Come, my son; come on, in God's name! I know
wherefore thy coming is. Oh, my son, my son! what cause
hath ever been that thou shouldst forsake me, and follow this
viled and reprobate company, which abuseth youth so mani-
festly? Oh, my son, thou knowest that these doings will end   5
thy father's days.

He weeps.

Ay, so, so, my son, thou fearest not to approach the presence
of thy sick father in that disguised sort. I tell thee, my son,
that there is never a needle in thy cloak but it is a prick to
my heart, and never an eyelet-hole but it is a hole to my   10
soul; and wherefore thou bringest that dagger in thy hand I
know not, but by conjecture.

He weeps.

Prince. [*Aside.*] My conscience accuseth me.—Most
sovereign lord, and well-beloved father, to answer first

to the last point, that is, whereas you conjecture that this   15
hand and this dagger shall be armed against your life, no!
Know, my beloved father, far be the thoughts of your son
—"son," said I? an unworthy son for so good a father!—
but far be the thoughts of any such pretended mischief. And
I most humbly render it [*giving him the dagger, kneeling*]   20
to your Majesty's hand. And live, my lord and sovereign,
for ever! And with your dagger-arm show like vengeance
upon the body of—"that, your son," I was about to say, and
dare not; ah, woe is me therefore!—that, your wild slave.
'Tis not the crown that I come for, sweet father, because I   25
am unworthy. And those "viled and reprobate" companions—I abandon and utterly abolish their company for ever!
Pardon, sweet father! pardon! the least thing and most desire. And this ruffianly cloak I here tear from my back, and
sacrifice it to the devil, which is master of all mischief.   30
Pardon me, sweet father, pardon me! Good my Lord of
Exeter, speak for me. Pardon me! pardon, good father! Not
a word? Ah, he will not speak one word! Ah, Harry, now
thrice-unhappy Harry! But what shall I do? I will go take
me into some solitary place, and there lament my sinful life;   35
and, when I have done, I will lay me down and die.

Exit.

King. Call him again! Call my son again!

[*Enter the* PRINCE.]

Prince. And doth my father call me again? Now, Harry,
happy be the time that thy father calleth thee again! [*He
kneels.*]   40
King. Stand up, my son; and do not think thy father but
at the request of thee, my son, I will pardon thee. And God
bless thee, and make thee his servant.

Prince. Thanks, good my lord. And no doubt but this day, even this day, I am born new again.   45

King. Come, my son and lords, take me by the hands.

Exeunt omnes.

[SCENE SEVEN.]

[*Outside John Cobbler's House.*]

Enter DERICK [*shouting at* MISTRESS COBBLER *within*].

Derick. Thou art a stinking whore! and a whoreson stinking whore! Dost think I'll take it at thy hands?

Enter JOHN COBBLER, *running.*

John. Derick, Derick, Derick, hearest thou? Do, Derick, never while thou livest use that! Why, what will my neighbore say and thou go away so?   5

Derick. She's a narrant whore; and I'll have the law on you, John.

John. Why, what hath she done?

Derick. Marry, mark thou, John. I will prove it, that I will!   10

John. What wilt thou prove?

Derick. That she called me in to dinner—John, mark the tale well, John—and when I was set, she brought me a dish of roots and a piece of barrel-butter therein! And she is a very knave, and thou a drab if thou take her part.   15

John. Hearest thou, Derick? Is this the matter? Nay, if it be no worse we will go home again, and all shall be amended.

Derick. Oh, John, hearest thou, John? Is all well?

John. Ay, all is well.   20

Derick. Then I'll go home before, and break all the glass windows.

[*Exeunt* DERICK *and* JOHN.]

[SCENE EIGHT.]

[*The Jerusalem Chamber, Westminster Palace, March 20, 1413.*]

Enter the KING *with his* LORDS [EXETER *and* OXFORD].

King. Come, my lords. I see it boots me not to take any physic, for all the physicians in the world cannot cure me; no, not one. But, good my lords, remember my last will and testament concerning my son; for truly, my lords, I do not think but he will prove as valiant and victorious a king as   5
ever reigned in England.

Both. Let heaven and earth be witness between us if we accomplish not thy will to the uttermost.

King. I give you most unfeigned thanks, good my lords. Draw the curtains, and depart my chamber awhile; and   10
cause some music to rock me a-sleep.

He sleeps. Exeunt LORDS.

Enter the PRINCE.

Prince. Ah, Harry, thrice-unhappy, that hath neglected so long from visiting of thy sick father! I will go. Nay, but why do I not go to the chamber of my sick father to comfort the melancholy soul of his body? His soul, said I? Here   15
is his body, indeed, but his soul is whereas it needs no body. Now, thrice-accursed Harry, that hath offended thy father so much! And could not I crave pardon for all? O my dying

father! Curst be the day wherein I was born, and accursed
be the hour wherein I was begotten! But what shall I do? If   20
weeping tears, which come too late, may suffice the negligence, neglected to some, I will weep day and night until the
fountain be dry with weeping.

Exit [*taking the crown*].

Enter LORD[s] OF EXETER *and* OXFORD.

Exeter. Come easily, my lord, for waking of the King.
King. [*Waking.*] Now, my lords?   25
Oxford. How doth your Grace feel your self?
King. Somewhat better after my sleep. But, good my
lords, take off my crown. Remove my chair a little back, and
set me right.
Both. If [it] please your Grace, the crown is taken   30
away.
King. The crown taken away! Good my Lord of Ox-
ford, go see who hath done this deed.

[*Exit* OXFORD.]

No doubt 'tis some viled traitor that hath done it to deprive
my son. They that would do it now would seek to scrape   35
and scrawl for it after my death.

Enter LORD OF OXFORD *with the* PRINCE.

Oxford. Here, if [it] please your Grace, is my lord the
young Prince with the crown.
King. Why, how now, my son? I had thought the last
time I had you in schooling I had given you a lesson for all;   40
and do you now begin again? Why, tell me, my son, dost
thou think the time so long that thou wouldst have it before
the breath be out of my mouth?
Prince. Most sovereign lord and well-beloved father, I

came into your chamber to comfort the melancholy soul of   45
your body; and finding you at that time past all recovery,
and dead, to my thinking—God is my witness—and what
should I do, but with weeping tears lament the death of you,
my father? And after that, seeing the crown, I took it. And
tell me, my father, who might better take it than I, after your   50
death? But, seeing you live, I most humbly render it into
your Majesty's hands [*giving him the crown, kneeling*];
and the happiest man alive that my father lives. And live, my
lord and father, for ever!

King. Stand up, my son. Thine answer hath sounded well   55
in mine ears; for I must need confess that I was in a very
sound sleep, and altogether unmindful of thy coming. But
come near, my son, and let me put thee in possession whilst
I live, that none deprive thee of it after my death.

Prince. Well may I take it at your Majesty's hands; but it   60
shall never touch my head so long as my father lives.

He takes the crown.

King. God give thee joy, my son. God bless thee, and
made thee his servant, and send thee a prosperous reign! For
God knows, my son, how hardly I came by it, and how
hardly I have maintained it.   65

Prince. Howsoever you came by it I know not; but now I
have it from you, and from you I will keep it. And he that
seeks to take the crown from my head, let him look that his
armor be thicker than mine, or I will pierce him to the heart,
were it harder than brass or bullion.   70

King. Nobly spoken, and like a king! Now trust me, my
lords, I fear not but my son will be as warlike and victorious
a prince as ever reigned in England.

Both lords. His former life shows no less.

King. Well, my lords, I know not whether it be for sleep,   75 or drawing near of drowsy summer of death, but I am very much given to sleep. Therefore, good my lords, and my son, draw the curtains; depart my chamber; and cause some music to rock me a-sleep.

Exeunt omnes.

The King dies.

[SCENE NINE.]

[*Outside Westminster Abbey, after the Coronation, April 9, 1413.*]

Enter the THIEF.

Thief. Ah, God, I am now much like to a bird which hath escaped out of the cage; for so soon as my Lord Chief Justice heard that the old King was dead he was glad to let me go for fear of my lord the young Prince. But here come some of his companions. I will see if I can get anything of them   5
for old acquaintance.

Enter KNIGHTS, *ranging.*

Tom. Gog's wounds, the King is dead!
Jockey. Dead! then, Gog's blood, we shall be all kings!
Ned. Gog's wounds, I shall be Lord Chief Justice of England.   10
Tom. [*To the* THIEF.] Why, how! Are you broken out of prison?
Ned. Gog's wounds, how the villain stinks!
Jockey. Why, what will become of thee now? Fie upon him, how the rascal stinks!   15
Thief. Marry, I will go and serve my master again.

Tom. Gog's blood, dost think that he will have any such scabbed knave as thou art? What, man! he is a king now.

Ned. [*Giving him money.*] Hold thee. Here's a couple of angels for thee. And get thee gone, for the King will not be   20
long before he come this way. And hereafter I will tell the King of thee.

Exit THIEF.

Jockey. Oh, how it did me good to see the King when he was crowned! Methought his seat was like the figure of heaven, and his person was like unto a god.   25

Ned. But who would have thought that the King would have changed his countenance so?

Jockey. Did you not see with what grace he sent his embassage into France to tell the French King that Harry of England hath sent for the crown, and Harry of England will   30
have it?

Tom. But 'twas but a little to make the people believe that he was sorry for his father's death.

The trumpet sounds.

Ned. Gog's wounds, the King comes! Let's all stand aside.   35

Enter the KING *with the* ARCHBISHOP [OF CANTERBURY], *and the* LORD OF OXFORD.

Jockey. How do you do, my lord?

Ned. How now, Harry? Tut, my lord, put away these dumps. You are a king, and all the realm is yours. What, man! do you not remember the old sayings? You know I must be Lord Chief Justice of England. Trust me, my lord,   40
methinks you are very much changed. And 'tis but with a

little sorrowing, to make folks believe the death of your
father grieves you—and 'tis nothing so.

King. I prithee, Ned, mend thy manners, and be more
modester in thy terms; for my unfeigned grief is not to be   45
ruled by thy flattering and dissembling talk. Thou sayst I
am changed; so I am, indeed; and so must thou be, and that
quickly, or else I must cause thee to be changed.

Jockey. Gog's wounds, how like you this? Zounds! 'tis
not so sweet as music.   50

Tom. I trust we have not offended your Grace no way.

King. Ah, Tom, your former life grieves me, and makes
me to abandon and abolish your company for ever. And
therefore, not upon pain of death to approach my presence
by ten miles space. Then, if I hear well of you, it may be I   55
will do somewhat for you; otherwise, look for no more
favor at my hands than at any other man's. And, therefore,
be gone! we have other matters to talk on.

Exeunt KNIGHTS.

King. Now, my good Lord Archbishop of Canterbury,
what say you to our embassage into France?   60

Archbishop. Your right to the French crown of France
came by your great grandmother Isabel, wife to King Edward the Third, and sister to Charles, the French king.
Now, if the French king deny it, as likely enough he will,
then must you take your sword in hand and conquer the   65
right. Let the usurped Frenchman know, although your
predecessors have let it pass, you will not; for your countrymen are willing with purse and men to aid you. Then, my
good lord, as it hath been always known that Scotland hath
been in league with France by a sort of pensions which   70
yearly come from thence, I think it therefore best to conquer Scotland; and then I think that you may go more

easily into France. And this is all that I can say, my good
lord.

  King. I thank you, my good Lord Archbishop of Canter-   75
bury. What say you, my good Lord of Oxford?

  Oxford. If [it] please your Majesty, I agree to my
Lord Archbishop, saving in this:—"He that will Scotland
win must first with France begin," according to the old saying. Therefore, my good lord, I think it best first to invade   80
France; for in conquering Scotland you conquer but one;
and conquer France and conquer both.

Enter LORD OF EXETER.

  Exeter. If [it] please your Majesty, my Lord Ambassador is come out of France.

  King. Now trust me, my lord, he was the last man that   85
we talked of. I am glad that he is come to resolve us of our
answer. Commit him to our presence.

Enter DUKE OF YORK.

  York. God save the life of my sovereign lord the King!

  King. Now, my good lord the Duke of York, what news
from our brother the French king?   90

  York. If [it] please your Majesty, I delivered him my
embassage, whereof I took some deliberation. But for the
answer, he hath sent my Lord Ambassador of Bourges, the
Duke of Burgundy, Monsieur le Cole, with two hundred
and fifty horsemen to bring the embassage.   95

  King. Commit my Lord Archbishop of Bourges into our
presence.

Enter ARCHBISHOP OF BOURGES.

  King. Now, my Lord Archbishop of Bourges, we do
learn by our Lord Ambassador that you have our message

to do from our brother the French king. Here, my good 100
lord, according to our accustomed order, we give you free
liberty and license to speak with good audience.

Archbishop. God save the mighty King of England! My
lord and master, the most Christian king, Charles the Seventh,
the great and mighty King of France, as a most noble and 105
Christian king not minding to shed innocent blood, is rather
content to yield somewhat to your unreasonable demands—
that, if fifty thousand crowns a year, with his daughter, the
said Lady Katherine, in marriage, and some crowns which
he may well spare not hurting of his kingdom, he is content 110
to yield so far to your unreasonable desire.

King. Why, then, belike your lord and master thinks to
puff me up with fifty thousands crowns a year? No! Tell
thy lord and master that all the crowns in France shall not
serve me, except the crown and kingdom itself! And per- 115
chance hereafter I will have his daughter.

Archbishop. If it please your Majesty, my Lord Prince
Dolphin greets you well with this present.

He delivers a tun of tennis balls.

King. What, a guilded tun! I pray you, my Lord of York,
look what is in it.   120

York. If it please your Grace, here is a carpet, and a
tun of tennis balls.

King. A tun of tennis balls! I pray you, good my Lord
Archbishop, what might the meaning thereof be?

Archbishop. If it please you, my lord, a messenger, you 125
know, ought to keep close his message—and especially an
ambassador.

King. But I know that you may declare your message to
a king; the Law of Arms allows no less.

Archbishop. My lord, hearing of your wildness before 130

your father's death, sent you this, my good lord, meaning
that you are more fitter for a tennis court than a field, and
more fitter for a carpet than the camp.

King. My Lord Prince Dolphin is very pleasant with me!
But tell him that instead of balls of leather we will toss him   135
balls of brass and iron—yea, such balls as never were tossed
in France. The proudest tennis court shall rue it! Ay, and
thou, Prince of Bourges, shalt rue it! Therefore, get thee
hence; and tell him thy message quickly, lest I be there be-
for thee. Away, priest! be gone!   140

Archbishop. I beseech your Grace to deliver me your
safe conduct under your broad seal emanuel.

King. Priest of Bourges, know that the hand and seal of a
king, and his word, is all one. And instead of my hand and
seal I will bring him my hand and sword. And tell thy lord   145
and master that I, Harry of England, said it; and I, Harry of
England, will perform it! My Lord of York, deliver him our
safe conduct under our broad seal emanuel.

Exeunt Archbishop *and the* Duke of York.

King. Now, my lords, to arms! For I vow by heaven and
earth that the proudest Frenchman in all France shall rue the   150
time that ever these tennis balls were sent into England. My
lord, I will that there be provided a great navy of ships with
all speed at Southampton, for there I mean to ship my men;
for I would be there before him, if it were possible. Therefore come—but stay! I had almost forgot the chiefest thing   155
of all with chafing with this French ambassador. Call in my
Lord Chief Justice of England.

Enter Lord Chief Justice of England.

Exeter. Here is the King, my lord.
Justice. God preserve your Majesty!

King. Why, how now, my lord? what is the matter?   160

Justice. I would it were unknown to your Majesty.

King. Why, what ails you?

Justice. Your Majesty knoweth my grief well.

King. Oh, my lord, you remember you sent me to the Fleet, did you not?   165

Justice. I trust your Grace have forgotten that.

King. Ay, truly, my lord; and for revengement I have chosen you to be my Protector over my realm, until it shall please God to give me speedy return out of France.

Justice. And if it please your Majesty, I am far unworthy   170 of so high a dignity.

King. Tut, my lord! you are not unworthy, because I think you worthy; for you that would not spare me, I think, will not spare another. It must needs be so. And therefore, come, let us be gone, and get our men in a readiness.   175

Exeunt omnes.

[Scene Ten.]

[*Outside John Cobbler's House.*]

Enter a Captain, John Cobbler, *and his* Wife.

Captain. Come, come; there's no remedy. Thou must needs serve the King.

John. Good master Captain, let me go. I am not able to go so far.

Wife. I pray you, good master Captain, be good to my   5 husband.

Captain. Why, I am sure he is not too good to serve the King.

John. Alas, no—but a great deal too bad; therefore, I pray you, let me go.   10

Captain. No, no; thou shalt go.

John. Oh, sir, I have a great many shoes at home to cobble.

Wife. I pray you, let him go home again.

Captain. Tush, I care not. Thou shalt go.   15

John. Oh, wife, if you had been a loving wife to me this had not been; for I have said many times that I would go away, and now I must go—against my will.

He weeps.

Enter DERICK [*with a pot-lid for a shield*].

Derick. How now, ho! *Basillus manus,* for an old cod-piece! Master Captain, shall we away? Zounds! How now,   20
John? What, a-crying? What make you and my dame there? [*To the wife.*] I marvel whose head you will throw the stools at now we are gone.

Wife. I'll tell you! Come, you cloghead! What do you with my pot-lid? Here you, will you have it rapped about   25
your pate?

She beats him with her pot-lid.

Derick. Oh good dame!

Here he shakes her.

Derick. If I had my dagger here I would worry you all to pieces—that I would!

Wife. Would you so? I'll try that.   30

She beats him.

Derick. Master Captain, will you suffer her? Go to, dame! [*He retreats.*] I will go back as far as I can; but, if you come again—I'll clap the law on your back, that's flat!

I'll tell you, Master Captain, what you shall do: press her for a soldier! I warrant you she will do as much good as her husband and I too.

Enter the THIEF.

Derick. Zounds! who comes yonder?

Captain. How now, good fellow; dost thou want a master?

Thief. Ay, truly, sir.

Captain. Hold thee, then. I press thee for a soldier to serve the King in France.

Derick. How now, "Gads"! What, dost know us, thinkest?

Thief. Ay, I knew thee long ago.

Derick. Hear you, Master Captain.

Captain. What sayst thou?

Derick. I pray you, let me go home again.

Captain. Why, what wouldst thou do at home?

Derick. Marry, I have brought two shirts with me, and I would carry one of them home again; for I am sure he'll steal it from me, he is such a filching fellow.

Captain. I warrant thee he will not steal it from thee. Come, let's away.

Derick. Come, Master Captain, let's away. Come, follow me.

John. Come, wife, let's part lovingly.

Wife. Farewell, good husband.

Derick. Fie, what a kissing and crying is here! Zounds, do you think he will never come again? Why, John, come away! Dost think that we are so base-minded to die among Frenchmen? Zounds, we know not whether they will lay us in their church or no. Come, Master Captain, let's away.

Captain. I cannot stay no longer; therefore, come away.

Exeunt omnes.

[SCENE ELEVEN.]

[*The French Court, Rouen.*]

Enter the [FRENCH] KING, PRINCE DOLPHIN, *and*
LORD HIGH CONSTABLE OF FRANCE.

King. Now, my Lord High Constable, what say you to
our embassage into England?

Constable. If it please your Majesty, I can say nothing
until my lords ambassadors be come home. But yet methinks
your Grace hath done well to get your men in so good a   5
readiness for fear of the worst.

King. Ay, my lord, we have some in a readiness; but if
the King of England make against us we must have thrice
so many more.

Dolphin. Tut, my lord; although the King of England   10
be young and wild-headed, yet never think he will be so
unwise to make battle against the mighty King of France.

King. Oh, my son, although the King of England be
young and wild-headed, yet never think but he is ruled by
his wise councilors.   15

Enter ARCHBISHOP OF BOURGES.

Archbishop. God save the life of my sovereign lord the
King!

King. Now, my good Lord Archbishop of Bourges, what
news from our brother, the English king?

Archbishop. If [it] please your Majesty, he is so far   20
from your expectation that nothing will serve him but the
crown and kingdom itself. Besides, he bade me haste quickly
lest he be there before me. And, so far as I hear, he hath kept
promise; for they say he is already landed at Kidocks in

Normandy upon the River Seine, and laid his siege to the   25
garrison-town of Harfleur.

King. You have made great haste in the meantime, have
you not?

Dolphin. I pray you, how did the King of England take
my presents?   30

Archbishop. Truly, my lord, in very ill part. For these
your balls of leather he will toss you balls of brass and iron.
Trust me, my lord, I was very afraid of him, he is such a
haughty and high-minded prince. He is as fierce as a lion.

Constable. Tush! we will make him as tame as a lamb, I   35
warrant you.

Enter a MESSENGER.

Messenger. God save the mighty King of France!

King. Now, messenger, what news?

Messenger. If it please your Majesty, I come from
your poor distressed town of Harfleur, which is so beset on   40
every side, if your Majesty do not send present aid the town
will be yielded to the English king.

King. Come, my lords, come! Shall we stand still till our
country be spoiled under our noses? My lords, let the Normans, Brabanters, Picards, and Danes be sent for with all   45
speed. And you, my Lord High Constable, I make General
over all my whole army; Monsieur le Colle, Master of the
Bows, Seigneur Devens, and all the rest, at your appointment.

Dolphin. I trust your Majesty will bestow some part of
the battle on me. I hope not to present any otherwise than   50
well.

King. I tell thee, my son, although I should get the victory, and thou lose thy life, I should think myself quite
conquered, and the Englishmen to have the victory.

Dolphin. Why, my lord and father, I would have the   55
petty king of England to know that I dare encounter him in
any ground of the world.

King. I know well, my son; but at this time I will have it
thus. Therefore, come away.

Exeunt omnes.

[SCENE TWELVE.]

[*The field at Agincourt, October 25, 1415.*]

Enter HENRY THE FIFTH, *with his* LORDS.

King. Come, my lords of England. No doubt this good
luck of winning this town is a sign of an honorable victory
to come! But, good my lord, go and speak to the captains
with all speed, to number the host of the Frenchmen, and
by that means we may the better know how to appoint the   5
battle.

York. If it please your Majesty, there are many of
your men sick and diseased, and many of them die for want
of victuals.

King. And why did you not tell me of it before? If we   10
cannot have it for money we will have it by dint of sword;
the Law of Arms allows no less.

Oxford. I beseech your Grace to grant me a boon.

King. What is that, my good lord?

Oxford. That your Grace would give me the vanguard   15
in the battle.

King. Trust me, my Lord of Oxford, I cannot; for I have
already given it to my uncle, the Duke of York. Yet I thank
you for your good will.

A trumpet sounds.

How now, what is that? 20
York. I think it be some herald of arms.

Enter a HERALD.

Herald. King of England, my Lord High Constable and
others of the noblemen of France send me to defy thee as
open enemy to God, our country, and us; and hereupon
they presently bid thee battle. 25
King. Herald, tell them that I defy them as open enemies
to God, my country, and me, and as wrongful usurpers of
my right. And whereas thou sayst they presently bid me
battle, tell them that I think they know how to please me.
But, I pray thee, what place hath my lord Prince Dolphin 30
here in battle?
Herald. If it please your Grace, my Lord and King,
his father, will not let him come into the field.
King. Why, then, he doth me great injury. I thought
that he and I should have played at tennis together; there- 35
fore I have brought tennis balls for him—but other manner
of ones than he sent me. And, Herald, tell my Lord Prince
Dolphin that I have inured my hands with other kind of
weapons than tennis balls ere this time of day, and that he
shall find it, ere it be long. And so, adieu, my friend. And 40
tell my lord that I am ready when he will.

Exit HERALD.

Come, my lords. I care not if I go to our captains; and I'll
see the number of the French army myself. Strike up the
drum!

Exeunt omnes.

[SCENE THIRTEEN.]

[*In the French Camp.*]

Enter FRENCH SOLDIERS.

First Soldier. Come away, Jack Drummer! Come away all, and me will tell you what me will do. Me will tro one shance on the dice who shall have the king of England and his lords.

Second Soldier. Come away, Jack Drummer, and tro   5
your shance; and lay down your drum.

Enter DRUMMER.

Drummer. Oh, the brave apparel that the English-mans hay broth over! I will tell you what me ha done. Me ha provided a hundreth trunks, and all to put the fine apparel of the English-mans in.   10

First Soldier. What do thou mean by "trunks"?

Second Soldier. A shest, man, a hundred shests.

First Soldier. Awee, awee, awee. Me will tell you what: me ha put five shildren out of my house, and all too little to put the fine apparel of the English-mans in.   15

Drummer. Oh, the brave, the brave apparel that we shall have anon! But come, and you shall see what me will tro at the king's drummer and fife. Ha! me ha no good luck. Tro you.

Third Soldier. Faith, me will tro at the Earl of Northum-   20
berland, and my Lord of Willoughby, with his great horse, snorting, farting—oh brave horse!

First Soldier. Ha! By our Lady, you ha reasonable good luck. Now I will tro at the King himself. Ha! me have no good luck.   25

Enter a CAPTAIN.

Captain. How now! what make you here so far from the camp?

Second Soldier. Shall me tell our captain what we have done here?

Drummer. Awee, awee.   30

Exeunt DRUMMER *and one* SOLDIER.

Second Soldier. I will tell you what we have done. We have been troing our shance on the dice; but none can win the King.

Captain. I think so. Why, he is left behind for me! And I have set three or four chair-makers a-work to make a new   35
disguised chair to set that womanly King of England in, that all the people may laugh and scoff at him.

Second Soldier. Oh brave captain!

Captain. I am glad, and yet with a kind of pity, to see the poor King—why, who ever saw a more flourishing army in   40
France in one day than here is? Are not here all the peers of France? Are not here the Normans, with their firey hand-guns and flaunching curtleaxes? Are not here the bar-barians, with their barded horses and launching spears? Are not here the Picards, with their cross-bows and piercing   45
darts? The men of Hainault, with their cutting glaives and sharp carbuncles? Are not here the lance-knights of Bur-gundy? And, on the other side, a site of poor English scabs! Why, take an English-man out of his warm bed and his stale drink but one month, and, alas! what will become of   50
him? But give the Frenchman a radish root, and he will live with it all the days of his life.

Exit.

Second Soldier. Oh, the brave apparel that we shall have
of the English-mans.

[*Exeunt omnes.*]

[SCENE FOURTEEN.]

[*Another part of the battlefield.*]

Enter the KING OF ENGLAND *and his* LORDS.

King. Come, my lords and fellows of arms. What company is there of the Frenchmen?

Oxford. If it please your Majesty, our captains have
numbered them, and, so near as they can judge, they are
about threescore thousand horsemen and forty thousand   5
footmen.

King. They threescore thousand horsemen, and we but
two thousand! They forty thousand footmen, and we twelve
thousand! They are a hundred thousand, and we fourteen
thousand! Ten to one! My lords and loving countrymen,   10
though we be few, and they many, fear not. Your quarrel is
good, and God will defend you. Pluck up your hearts, for
this day we shall either have a valiant victory, or an honorable death! Now, my lords, I will that my uncle, the Duke
of York, have the vanguard in the battle; the Earl of Derby, 15
the Earl of Oxford, the Earl of Kent, the Earl of Nottingham, the Earl of Huntingdon I will have beside the army,
that they may come fresh upon them; and I myself, with the
Duke of Bedford, the Duke of Clarence, and the Duke of
Gloucester will be in the midst of the battle. Furthermore,   20
I will that my Lord of Willoughby and the Earl of Northumberland, with their troops of horsemen, be continually
running like wings on both sides of the army—my Lord of

Northumberland on the left wing. Then I will that every
archer provide him a stake of a tree, and sharpen it at both   25
ends; and, at the first encounter of the horsemen, to pitch
their stakes down into the ground before them, that they
may gore themselves upon them; and then, to recoil back,
and shoot wholly altogether, and so discomfit them.

Oxford. If it please your Majesty, I will take that in   30
charge, if your Grace be therewith content.

King. With all my heart, my good Lord of Oxford. And
go and provide quickly.

Oxford. I thank your Highness.

Exit.

King. Well, my lords, our battles are ordained, and the   35
French making of bonfires, and at their banquets. But let
them look, for I mean to set upon them.

The trumpet sounds.

Soft, here comes some other French message.

Enter HERALD.

Herald. King of England, my Lord High Constable and
others of my lords, considering the poor estate of thee and   40
thy poor countrymen, send me to know what thou wilt give
for thy ransom. Perhaps thou mayst agree better cheap now
than when thou art conquered.

King. Why then, belike, your High Constable sends to
know what I will give for my ransom? Now trust me,   45
Herald, not so much as a tun of tennis balls—no, not so much
as one poor tennis ball! Rather shall my body lie dead in the
field to feed crows than ever England shall pay one penny
ransom for my body.

Herald. A kingly resolution!   50

King. No, Herald; 'tis a kingly resolution and the resolution of a king. Here, take this for thy pains.

Exit HERALD.

King. But stay, my lords; what time is it?
All. Prime, my lord.
King. Then is it good time, no doubt, for all England   55
prayeth for us. What, my lords! methinks you look cheerfully upon me. Why, then, with one voice, and like true English hearts, with me throw up your caps, and for England cry, "Saint George!" And God and Saint George help us!   60

Let the DRUMMER *strike.*

Exeunt omnes.

[SCENE FIFTEEN.]

[*Another part of the battlefield.*]

The Frenchmen cry within, "Saint Denis! Saint Denis! Mount Joy! Saint Denis!"

The battle.

Enter KING OF ENGLAND *and his* LORDS.

King. Come, my lords, come! By this time our swords are almost drunk with French blood. But, my lords, which of you can tell me how many of our army be slain in the battle?
Oxford. If it please your Majesty, there are of the   5
French army slain above ten thousand twenty-six hundred, whereof are princes and nobles bearing banners; besides, all the nobility of France are taken prisoners. Of your

Majesty's army are slain none but the good Duke of York, and not above five or six and twenty common soldiers.   10

King. For the good Duke of York, my uncle, I am heartily sorry, and greatly lament his misfortune. Yet the honorable victory which the Lord hath given us doth make me much rejoice. But, stay! here comes another French message.   15

Sound trumpet.

Enter a HERALD, *and kneels.*

Herald. God save the life of the most mighty conqueror, the honorable King of England!

King. Now, Herald, methinks the world is changed with you now. What! I am sure it is a great disgrace for a herald to kneel to the King of England! What is thy message?   20

Herald. My lord and master, the conquered King of France, sends thee long health, with hearty greeting.

King. Herald, his greetings are welcome; but I thank God for my health. Well, Herald, say on.

Herald. He hath sent me to desire your Majesty to give   25
him leave to go into the field to view his poor countrymen, that they may all be honorably buried.

King. Why, Herald, doth thy lord and master send to me to bury the dead? Let him bury them, in God's name! But, I pray thee, Herald, where is my Lord High Constable, and   30
those that would have had my ransom?

Herald. If it please your Majesty, he was slain in the battle.

King. Why, you may see—you will make your selves sure before the victory be won. But, Herald, what castle is this   35
so near adjoining to our camp?

Herald. If it please your Majesty, 'tis called the Castle of Agincourt.

King. Well then, my lords of England, for the more honor of our Englishmen, I will that this be forever called   40
The Battle of Agincourt.

Herald. If it please your Majesty, I have a further message to deliver to your Majesty.

King. What is that, Herald? Say on.

Herald. If it please your Majesty, my lord and master   45
craves to parley with your Majesty.

King. With a good will—so some of my nobles view the place for fear of treachery and treason.

Herald. Your Grace need not to doubt that.

King. Well, tell him, then, I will come.   50

Exit HERALD.

Now, my lords, I will go into the field myself to view my countrymen, and to have them honorably buried; for the French king shall never surpass me in courtesy whiles I am Harry, King of England. Come on, my lords.

Exeunt omnes.

[SCENE SIXTEEN.]

[*Another part of the battlefield.*]

Enter JOHN COBBLER *and* ROBIN PEWTERER.

Robin. Now, John Cobbler, didst thou see how the King did behave himself?

John. But, Robin, didst thou see what a policy the King had? To see how the Frenchmen were killed with the stakes of the trees!   5

Robin. Ay, John, there was a brave policy!

Enter an English Soldier, *roaming.*

Soldier. What are you, my masters?
Both. Why, we be Englishmen.
Soldier. Are you Englishmen? Then change your language, for the King's tents are set afire, and all they that   10
speak English will be killed.

[*Exit* Soldier.]

John. What shall we do, Robin? Faith, I'll shift, for I can
speak broken French.
Robin. Faith, so can I. Let's hear how thou canst speak.
John. Commodevales, Monsieur?   15
Robin. That's well. Come, let's be gone.

[*Exeunt.*]

[Scene Seventeen.]

[*Another part of the battlefield.*]

Drum and trumpet sound.

Enter Derick, *roaming. After him a* Frenchman,
and takes him prisoner.

Derick. Oh, good *Mounser!*
Frenchman. Come, come, you *villiago!*
Derick. Oh, I will, sir, I will.
Frenchman. Come quickly, you peasant!
Derick. I will, sir. What shall I give you?   5
Frenchman. Marry, thou shalt give me one, two, tre, four
hundred crowns.
Derick. Nay, sir, I will give you more; I will give as
many crowns as will lie on your sword.

Frenchman. Wilt thou give me as many crowns as will lie   10
on my sword?

Derick. Ay, marry, will I. Ay, but you must lay down
your sword, or else they will not lie on your sword.

Here the FRENCHMAN *lays down his sword, and the* CLOWN
[DERICK] *takes it up, and hurls him down.*

Derick. Thou villain! darest thou look up?

Frenchman. Oh, good *Monsieur, comparteve! Monsieur,*   15
pardon me!

Derick. O you villain! now lie at my mercy. Dost thou
remember since thou lamedst me in thy short ell? O villain!
Now I will strike off thy head.

Here, whiles he turns his back, the FRENCHMAN *runs his
ways.*

Derick. What, is he gone? Mass, I am glad of it. For, if he   20
had stayed, I was afraid he would have stirred again, and
then I should have been spilt. But I will away to kill more
Frenchmen.

[*Exit.*]

[SCENE EIGHTEEN.]

[*Another part of the battlefield.*]

Enter KING OF FRANCE, KING OF ENGLAND, *and*
ATTENDANTS.

King of England. Now, my good brother of France, my
coming into this land was not to shed blood, but for the
right of my country; which, if you can deny, I am content
peaceably to leave my siege and to depart out of your land.

King of France. What is it you demand, my loving   5
brother of England?

King of England. My secretary hath it written. Read it.

Secretary. Item, that immediately Henry of England be
crowned King of France.

King of France. A very hard sentence, my good brother   10
of England.

King of England. No more but right, my good brother
of France!

King of France. Well, read on.

Secretary. Item, that after the death of the said Henry   15
the crown remain to him and his heirs forever.

King of France. Why then, you do not only mean to dis-
possess me, but also my son!

King of England. Why, my good brother of France, you
have had it long enough. And as for Prince Dolphin, it skills   20
not though he sit beside the saddle. Thus I have set it down,
and thus it shall be!

King of France. You are very peremptory, my good
brother of England.

King of England. And you as perverse, my good brother   25
of France.

King of France. Why then, belike all that I have here is
yours!

King of England. Ay, even as far as the kingdom of
France reaches.   30

King of France. Ay, for by this hot beginning we shall
scarce bring it to a calm ending.

King of England. It is as you please. Here is my resolution.

King of France. Well, my brother of England, if you   35
will give me a copy we will meet you again to-morrow.

King of England. With a good will, my good brother of France. Secretary, deliver him a copy.

Exit KING OF FRANCE *and all their* ATTENDANTS.

King of England. My lords of England, go before, and I will follow you.   40

Exeunt LORDS.

Speaks to himself.

King of England. Ah, Harry, thrice-unhappy Harry! Hast thou now conquered the French king, and beginst a fresh supply with his daughter? But with what face canst thou seek to gain her love which hath sought to win her father's crown? Her father's crown, said I? No, it is mine   45
own.

Ay, but I love her, and must crave her—
Nay, I love her, and will have her!

Enter LADY KATHERINE *and her* LADIES.

King of England. But here she comes. How now, fair Lady Katherine of France, what news?   50
Katherine. If it please your Majesty, my father sent me to know if you will debate any of these unreasonable demands which you require.
King of England. Now trust me, Kate, I commend thy father's wit greatly in this; for none in the world could   55
sooner have made me debate it, if it were possible. But tell me, sweet Kate, canst thou tell how to love?
Katherine. I cannot hate, my good lord; therefore, far unfit were it for me to love.
King of England. Tush, Kate! but tell me in plain terms,   60
canst thou love the King of England? I cannot do as these

countries do that spend half their time in wooing. Tush, wench, I am none such. But, wilt thou go over to England?

Katherine. I would to God that I had your Majesty as fast in love as you have my father in wars! I would not vouchsafe so much as one look until you had abated all these unreasonable demands.

King of England. Tush, Kate! I know thou wouldst not use me so hardly. But tell me, canst thou love the King of England?

Katherine. How should I love him that hath dealt so hardly with my father?

King of England. But I'll deal as easily with thee as heart can imagine, or tongue can require. How sayst thou? What! will it be?

Katherine. If I were of my own direction I could give you answer; but seeing I stand at my father's direction, I must first know his will.

King of England. But shall I have thy good will in the mean season?

Katherine. Whereas I can put your Grace in no assurance, I would be loath to put you in any despair.

King of England. Now, before God, it is a sweet wench!

She goes aside, and speaks as follows.

Katherine. I may think myself the happiest in the world that is beloved of the mighty King of England!

King of England. Well, Kate, are you at host with me? Sweet Kate, tell thy father from me that none in the world could sooner have persuaded me to it than thou; and so tell thy father from me.

Katherine. God keep your Majesty in good health.

Exit KATHERINE.

King of England. Farewell, sweet Kate. In faith, it is a
sweet wench! But if I knew I could not have her father's
good will, I would so rouse the towers over his ears that I
would make him be glad to bring her me upon his hands and
knees.   95

Exit KING.

[SCENE NINETEEN.]

[*Another part of the battlefield.*]

Enter DERICK *with his girdle full of shoes.*

Derick. How, now! Zounds, it did me good to see how I
did triumph over the Frenchmen!

Enter JOHN COBBLER, *roving, with a pack full of apparel.*

John. Whoop, Derick! How dost thou?
Derick. What, John! *Comedevales?* Alive yet?
John. I promise thee, Derick, I scaped hardly; for I was   5
within half a mile when one was killed!
Derick. Were you so?
John. Ay, trust me. I had like been slain.
Derick. But, once killed—why it—'tis nothing. I was four
or five times slain.   10
John. Four or five times slain. Why, how couldst thou
have been alive now?
Derick. O John, never say so! For I was called "the
bloody soldier" amongst them all.
John. Why, what didst thou?   15
Derick. Why, I will tell thee, John. Every day when I
went into the field I would take a straw and thrust it into

my nose and make my nose bleed; and then I would go into the field. And when the captain saw me, he would say, "Peace, a bloody soldier!" and bid me stand aside. Whereof   20
I was glad. But mark the chance, John: I went and stood behind a tree—but mark, then, John—I thought I had been safe; but on a sudden there steps to me a lusty, tall Frenchman; now he drew, and I drew; now I lay here, and he lay there; now I set this leg before, and turned this backward—   25
and skipped quite over a hedge; and he saw me no more there that day! And was not this well done, John?

John. By the mass, Derick, thou hast a witty head.

Derick. Ay, John, thou mayst see, if thou hadst taken my counsel. But what hast thou there? I think thou hast   30
been robbing the Frenchmen.

John. In faith, Derick, I have gotten some reparel to carry home to my wife.

Derick. And I have got some shoes; for I'll tell thee what I did: when they were dead, I would go take off all their   35
shoes.

John. Ay, but Derick, how shall we get home?

Derick. Nay, zounds, if they take thee they will hang thee. O, John, never do so! If it be thy fortune to be hanged, be hanged in thy own language, whatsoever thou dost!   40

John. Why, Derick, the wars is done; we may go home now.

Derick. Ay, but you may not go before you ask the King leave. But I know a way to go home and ask the King no leave.   45

John. How is that, Derick?

Derick. Why, John, thou knowest the Duke of York's funeral must be carried into England, dost thou not?

John. Ay, that I do.

Derick. Why, then, thou knowest we'll go with it.   50
John. Ay, but Derick, how shall we do for to meet them?
Derick. Zounds, if I make not shift to meet them, hang
me! Sirrah, thou knowest that in every town there will be
ringing, and there will be cakes and drink. Now I will go to
the clerk and sexton, and keep a-talking and say, "Oh, this   55
fellow rings well!" And thou shalt go and take a piece of
cake. Then I'll ring, and thou shalt say, "Oh, this fellow
keeps a good stint!" And then I will go drink to thee all the
way. But I marvel what my dame will say when we come
home, because we have not a French word to cast at a dog   60
by the way.
John. Why, what shall we do, Derick?
Derick. Why, John, I'll go before and call my dame
whore; and thou shalt come after and set fire on the house.
We may do it, John, for I'll prove it—because we be soldiers.   65

The trumpets sound.

John. Derick, help me to carry my shoes and boots.

[*Exeunt* DERICK *and* JOHN.]

[SCENE TWENTY.]

[*Another part of the battlefield.*]

Enter KING OF ENGLAND, LORDS OF OXFORD *and* EXETER,
then the KING OF FRANCE, PRINCE DOLPHIN, *and the* DUKE
OF BURGUNDY, PRINCESS KATHERINE *and* ATTENDANTS.

King of England. Now, my good brother of France, I
hope by this time you have deliberated of your answer.
King of France. Ay, my well-beloved brother of England. We have viewed it over with our learned council, but

cannot find that you should be crowned King of France.   5

King of England. What! not King of France? Then
nothing. I must be King. But, my loving brother of France,
I can hardly forget the late injuries offered me when I came
last to parley; the Frenchmen had better have raked the
bowels out of their fathers' carcasses than to have fired my   10
tents. And if I knew thy son Prince Dolphin, for one, I
would so rouse him as he was never so roused!

King of France. I dare swear for my son's innocency in
this matter. But if this please you, that immediately you be
proclaimed and crowned Heir and Regent of France, not   15
King, because I myself was once crowned king—

King of England. Heir and Regent of France? That is
well. But that is not all that I must have.

King of France. The rest my secretary hath in writing.

Secretary. [*Reads.*] Item, that Henry, King of England,   20
be crowned Heir and Regent of France during the life of
King Charles; and after his death the crown with all rights to
remain to King Henry of England, and to his heirs forever.

King of England. Well, my good brother of France,
there is one thing I must needs desire.   25

King of France. What is that, my good brother of England?

King of England. That all your nobles must be sworn to
be true to me.

King of France. Whereas they have not stuck with   30
greater matters, I know they will not stick with such a trifle.
Begin you, my Lord Duke of Burgundy.

King of England. Come, my Lord of Burgundy; take
your oath upon my sword.

Burgundy. I, Philip, Duke of Burgundy, swear to Henry,   35
King of England, to be true to him, and to become his liege

man; and that if I, Philip, hear of any foreign power coming to invade the said Henry, or his heirs, then I, the said Philip, to send him word, and aid him with all the power I can make. And thereunto I take my oath. 40

He kisses the sword.

King of England. Come, Prince Dolphin, you must swear, too.

He kisses the sword.

King of England. Well, my brother of France, there is one thing more I must needs require of you.

King of France. Wherein is it that we may satisfy your 45 Majesty?

King of England. A trifle, my good brother of France; I mean to make your daughter Queen of England, if she be willing, and you therewith content. How sayst thou, Kate? Canst thou love the King of England? 50

Katherine. How should I love thee, which is my father's enemy?

King of England. Tut! stand not upon these points. 'Tis you must make us friends. I know, Kate, thou art not a little proud that I love thee. What, wench, the King of England? 55

King of France. Daughter, let nothing stand betwixt the King of England and thee. Agree to it.

Katherine. [*Aside.*] I had best whilst he is willing, lest when I would he will not—I rest at your Majesty's command. 60

King of England. Welcome, sweet Kate! But, my brother of France, what say you to it?

King of France. With all my heart I like it. But when shall be your wedding day?

King of England. The first Sunday of the next month,   65
God willing.

Sound trumpets.

Exeunt omnes.

FINIS.

EXPLANATORY NOTES

TITLE. Probably suggested by the third chapter heading in Hall's chronicle: "The Victorious Acts of King Henry the Fifth"; cf. also Stow (1580), p. 581: "He [Henry of Monmouth] obtained grace of our Lord to attain to great victories and many glorious and incredible conquests." It was perhaps echoed by Elizabeth at Tilbury when just before the arrival of the Spanish Armada (July, 1588) she promised her army, "We shall shortly have a famous victory." Cf. Cheney, p. 411. The Folger Library possesses an anonymous tract entitled *A Famous Victory achieved in August last 1613 by the Christian Gallies of Sicilia against the Turks,* and another by Sir William Waller, *A Famous Victory obtained against the Cavaliers in the County of Gloucestershire . . . 1643.* The phrase had attained cliché status by the end of the eighteenth century; cf. Southey, *The Battle of Blenheim* (1798).

SUBTITLE. May be intended to distinguish the play from others in which the same hero figured; see p. 168.

Scene One

[. . . *Eve of St. John Baptist, 1410.*] See App. A, Scenes 2 and 3.
Ned and *Tom.* Sometimes designated as "Knights" by the original
  stage directions. (According to Stow, the Prince was accom-

panied by "young lords and gentlemen"; see App. A, Scene 1.)
Ned Poins of *1* and *2 Henry IV* probably derives from this Ned.

9. *a villainous part of me:* villainous on my part.
10. *receivers.* Officers charged with collecting taxes, perhaps attached to the king as pursuivants, i.e., attendants. See below, note on [*Exeunt Receivers.*].
15. *Sir John Oldcastle [Jockey].* See pp. 177–78.
16. *Zounds:* God's wounds. Cf. "Gog's wounds" (in line 61, and elsewhere).
18. *as passeth:* as passeth belief (?).
22. *the villain that was wont to spy out our booties.* A "setter" of "matches," in the language of *1 Henry IV*, I, 2, 119; II, 2, 53.
26. *it skills not:* it makes no difference. Cf. p. 159.
34. *this month:* for some time. Cf. p. 158.
[*Exeunt Receivers.*] The texts of 1598 and 1617 read *Exit Purseuant;* J. Q. Adams: *Exit Purseuant[s]*. The Receivers were presumably meant.
78. *feared:* terrified.
79. *our old host's at Faversham.* A topical reference (?). See p. 180.
83. *the old tavern in Eastcheap.* Doubtless a reference to the Boar's Head, but Stow (1603), I, 217, notes that in the fifteenth century there was no tavern in Eastcheap: "Of old time when friends did meet there, and were disposed to be merry, they went not to dine and sup in taverns, but to the cooks, where they called for meat what them liked, which they always found ready dressed at a reasonable rate."
89. *fellows:* equals.

Scene Two

Enter John Cobbler, Robin Pewterer, Lawrence Costermonger. Fleay, p. 67, proposed that these characters get their names, respectively, from the three Queen's men who, he thought, may have played them: John Laneham, Robert Wilson, and Lawrence Dutton.

4–5. *Pudding Lane, Billingsgate Ward.* Familiar names of places in Elizabethan London, near Eastcheap.
13. *toward:* bold.
14. *let:* hesitate.

19. *use it:* continue the practice.

roving: running hither and yon. Derick is in pursuit of the Thief.

34. *him.* Robin stupidly mistakes Derick for the Thief.

40. *his.* Robin's.

48. *him.* The Thief.

52. *it.* His dagger. Clowns commonly wore daggers; cf. *Friar Bacon and Friar Bungay*, Scene 1, lines 31–34: "Marry, sirrah Ned, thou shalt put on my cap and my coat and my dagger, and I will put on thy clothes and thy sword; and so thou shalt be my fool."

60. *'Tis a wonderful thing to see. . . .* Cf. "It is a wonderful thing to see . . ." (*2 Henry IV*, v, 1, 72). [*Monaghan.*]

66. *"Gad's Hill."* Derick does not know the Thief's name (Cutbert Cutter); he accordingly nicknames him after a place notorious for holdups: a hill on the Rochester highway, twenty miles southeast of London; cf. Hemingway, pp. 38, 42.

69. *taking:* thieving.

70. *bots.* A disease of horses.

71. *knocked:* slugged. Cf. *Two Gentlemen of Verona*, ii, 4, 7: " 'Twere good you knocked him."

74. *what make you:* what are you doing.

94. *the Counter.* A prison attached to the Mayor's court in London, from which the Prince would be released upon payment of damages.

97–112. The narratives of the Vintner's Boy and the Mayor (Scene 3) are based on Stow (see App. A, Scenes 2 and 3). Although there are similar accounts in Stow's *Summary of English Chronicles* both before and after 1580, only the *Chronicles* of that date associates the story with "the King's son," allowing the dramatist to relate it to Prince Henry. Prior to 1580, Stow had told the story specifically of Prince John, Henry's brother; afterwards (in 1590, etc.) he names either John or Princes Thomas and John. It is almost certain that the version of 1580 was the dramatist's source; but see Facts and Inferences, n. 55.

99. *good store:* aplenty.

99–100. *noise:* a band of musicians; see also Scene 4, line 88, and Scene 5, line 107; cf. *2 Henry IV*, ii, 4, 12: "Sneak's noise." Prince Henry's love of music had been noted by Stow, following Titus Livius; see App. A, Scene 1.

118. *till the sessions day:* till the court is in session.

121. *Newgate.* A famous London prison, 1218–1902.

123. [*To Derick.*] [*J. Q. Adams.*]

Scene Three

10. *give occasion:* give cause for annoyance. Cf. p. 158.
25. *liked them not:* displeased them.
29. *space of half an hour.* The Mayor and the Vintner's Boy agree as to the beginnings and duration of the quarrel. For the rest, the Boy's version is appropriately vague; see p. 110.
38. *sent him to ward:* imprisoned him.

Scene Four

[. . . *King's Bench.*] The supreme court of common law jurisdiction in England.
the Lord Chief Justice. Sir William Gascoigne (1350?–1419). We have record of a performance in which Richard Tarlton played the role of the Justice, in the absence of the actor to whom the part had been assigned; see p. 180.

16. *and have it in writing:* since you have it in your records.
21–23. *the 20th day of May last past, in the fourteenth year of the reign of our sovereign lord King Henry the Fourth.* B. M. Ward (1928, *R.E.S.*), p. 285, points out that "The fourteenth year of King Henry IV commenced on September 30, 1412, and ended with the King's death on March 20, 1413." Since the text is consequently erroneous, he feels free to postulate an arbitrary reference to an Elizabethan event. On May 20, 1573, according to their letter of complaint to Lord Burleigh, William Faust and John Wotton were attacked "by three of my Lord Oxford's men" at their lodgings in London, and the next day this was repeated as they were "riding peaceably by the highway, from Gravesend to Rochester" and "with full intent to murder us." The precise mention of May 20 and the location of the robbery near Gad's Hill (i.e., between Gravesend and Rochester) persuade Ward that the Earl himself dramatized this material shortly after the assault upon Faust and Wotton, in 1573, to provide frolicsome apology for his presumed participation, with Prince Henry's precedent, in crime on the highways. It may be observed, however, that, although Oxford's men were involved in the affair, there is no evidence he was one of the company. Also, the highway attack took place on May 21, not on May 20.

Ward overlooks the egregious reputation of Gad's Hill; see note on Scene 2, line 66. He brushes aside A. W. Pollard's comment to him that *The Famous Victories* must have been written somewhat later, since its author employs Stow's *Chronicles* (1580); see note on Scene 2, lines 97–112. In conclusion Ward asserts: "I do not for a moment suggest that Lord Oxford wrote the play in the version that Thomas Creede printed in 1598. But I think it quite possible that he wrote—and perhaps acted in—a Court masque in 1574; that this masque was afterwards modified to meet the requirements of the public stage in the 'eighties; and that in the 'nineties Shakespeare based upon it his famous trilogy." In his biography of Oxford, Ward, p. 366, n. 2, tacitly relinquishes his claim for the Earl's authorship of *The Famous Victories*.

37. *whether you will:* if it makes no difference to you.

Enter the young Prince. . . . The King has presumably effected his release from the Counter.

60. *quality:* nature.

80. *case me no casings:* don't mention his "case" to me. Cf. p. 136.

96. *in this place:* in the King's Court.

97. *lively:* actual.

99. *the Fleet.* A debtors' prison, abolished in 1845. Apropos of Falstaff's being remanded to the Fleet, Wilson (1944), p. 119, remarks that: "The Fleet was a prison of a special kind, used by the Privy Council, as well as by other government courts or officials, for the temporary custody of persons summoned before them for enquiry, whom they could not at the moment deal with."

104. *the prisoner.* Cutbert Cutter.

143. *mass:* by the mass.

147. *course you:* keep up with you (as in a race); cf. *The Taming of the Shrew*, INDUCTION, 2, 49: "Say thou wilt course. Thy grayhounds are as swift as breathèd stags . . ."

Exit. And straight enters again. Derick (as Prince) exits and returns as himself. John remains under the spell of the play. See p. 106.

151. *Worenday.* Unexplained.

166. *ringed.* Like a pig.

170. *crab:* crabapple.

171–72. *With nut-brown ale/That is full stale.* . . . Cf. "A cup of wine that's brisk and fine . . ." (*2 Henry IV*, v, 3, 48). [*Monaghan.*]

Scene Five

Enter the young Prince. . . . No doubt the King has once again intervened in his behalf.

25. *fence-schools.* Particularly fashionable in the 1580's. On October 24, 1587, Richard Tarlton, "ordinary groom of Her Majesty's Chamber," took the highest degree (Master of Fence) in such a school; cf. Halliwell-Phillips (1844), pp. xi–xii.

73. *tables:* memory. Ned does not need an actual notebook. Nor does Hamlet (1, 5, 107); Cf. p. 137.

82. *I had thought once-whiles I had lived to have seen:* I used to think that once while I lived I should see.

94. *rule:* conduct.

103. *countenance:* mark of favor.

106. *three noise of musicians:* a band of three musicians; see note on Scene 2, lines 99–100.

Scene Six

4. *viled:* wretched.

8. *disguised sort:* unaccustomed fashion (?). Whereas Stow (1580), p. 576, follows Titus Livius in relating that the Prince "disguised himself," Holinshed (1577), II, 1160a, corrects their source: "he appareled himself." Perhaps the garb was simply an extravagant costume of the historical Henry; cf. Chaucer, *Romance of the Rose*, lines 839–40:

> Wrought was his robe in straunge gise,
> And al toslytered for queyntise.

13. *[Aside.] [J. Q. Adams.]*

28. *pardon! the least thing and most desire:* pardon is the very small thing I ask of you and what I most desire.

39–40. *[He kneels.] [J. Q. Adams.]*

41–42. *do not think thy father but at the request of thee, my son, I will pardon thee:* do not think, my son, but that thy father at thy request will pardon thee.

45. *born new again.* Hall, f. HV, i, *recto:* "This King . . . determined to put on the shape of a new man . . ." Cf. John 3:3; I Pet. 1:23.

Scene Seven

4. *use that:* behave that way.
6. *a narrant:* an arrant. Cf. p. 161.

Scene Eight

12–13. *neglected so long.* At least two months, according to Stow, had elapsed since the Prince's reformation.
21–22. *suffice the negligence, neglected to some:* render satisfaction for the neglect I have shown toward some people. Cf. *King Lear,* I, I, 282: "You have obedience scanted/And well are worth the want which you have wanted."
22–23. *the fountain:* his eyes. Cf. p. 147.
. . . [*taking the crown.*] What happens is perfectly clear even without comment from the Prince. See pp. 196–97.
25. [*Waking.*] [*J. Q. Adams.*]
36. *scrawl:* scramble.
53. *and the happiest:* and I am the happiest.
67. *from you I will keep it:* having received it from you, I will keep it.
76. *summer:* slumber (?).

Scene Nine

ranging: roaming.
20. *angels.* Gold coins.
24. *seat:* posture. Cf. p. 150.
38. *these dumps:* this fit of melancholy. Cf. p. 140.
43. *nothing so:* not so at all.
133. *for a carpet:* for dancing. See p. 138.
134–36. *My Lord Prince Dolphin is very pleasant with me! But tell him that instead of balls of leather we will toss him balls of brass and iron. . . ."* Cf. "We are glad that Dauphin is so pleasant with us. . . . And tell the pleasant Prince this mock of his hath turned his balls to gunstones . . ." (*Henry V,* I, 2, 259–82). [*Monaghan.*]
142. *seal emanuel.* Cf. Hall, f. HV, x, *verso:* "seale and signe manuell." See pp. 136–37.

Scene Ten

3. *go . . . go:* leave . . . walk.
11. *go:* join the army.
[*with a pot-lid for a shield*]. [*J. Q. Adams.*]
19. Basillus manus, *for an old codpiece.* An uncomplimentary, vaguely obscene greeting. Corrupted from Spanish *besar los manos* (to kiss the hands, in greeting). [*J. Q. Adams.*]
22. [*To the wife.*] [*J. Q. Adams.*]
24. *cloghead:* with a clod for a head.
33. *clap the law:* clapperclaw (i.e., claw). Cf. p. 135.
42. "*Gads.*" Derick's abbreviation of "Gad's Hill," the nickname used in Scene 2, line 66.
49. *two shirts with me.* Cf. "I take but two shirts out with me" (*2 Henry IV*, I, 2, 234). [*Monaghan.*]

Scene Eleven

12. *unwise to:* unwise as to.
24. *Kidocks:* Kyd Caux [*Hall*]; Kedecaux [*Stow*]. Modern Cauxville (?).
34. *high-minded:* proud.
44-45. *Normans, Brabanters, Picards, and Danes.* Perhaps this list is intentionally ridiculous, suggesting the King's vague sense of his northwestern dominions.
47-48. *Monsieur le Colle . . . Seigneur Devens.* Topical references familiar to a Court audience (?).

Scene Twelve

2. *this town:* Harfleur. The siege occurred in August, 1415.
10. *If we cannot have it* (i.e., the battle), etc. The King does not wait for an answer to his question. Either it was perfunctory, or his conscience tender. He has elsewhere (as Prince) shifted the subject evasively; see Scene 1, line 12.
21. *herald of arms.* The phrase (no doubt commonplace) is played upon in *1 Henry VI*, I, 1, 45-46: "*Heralds*, wait on us./Instead of gold, we'll offer up our *arms*." See App. B, Item XIV.
42. *I care not if I go:* I'd rather like to go.

Scene Thirteen

15. *fine apparel of the English-mans.* A jibe at the extravagant dress of Elizabethan courtiers (?).
35–36. *new disguised:* in the latest fashion (?). See note on Scene 6, line 8.
 chair: chariot, according to the chronicles. Cf. *Henry V*, III, 54–55: "And in a captive chariot into Rouen/Bring him our prisoner."
43. *flaunching:* flaunting (?) (showy, gay). [*J. Q. Adams.*]
 curtleaxes: cutlasses.
 barbarians: Brabantians (?). Cf. Scene 11, line 45.
44. *barded:* covered with bards (leather plates of armor).
46. *glaives:* broadswords.
47. *carbuncles:* spikes at the center of shields.
48. *site:* quantity.

Scene Fourteen

1. *fellows:* comrades.
14–22. For these names, anachronistic and otherwise, see pp. 182–92.
32. In Stow (1580), p. 594, this task is assigned to the Duke of York. See p. 184.
51. *'tis a kingly resolution and the resolution of a king:* a resolution not only suitable for a king but in fact taken by a king.
54. *Prime:* 6:00 A.M.

Scene Sixteen

10–11. *all they that speak English will be killed.* The French have set the English camp afire. The Soldier thinks the day is lost. Cf. Hall (see App. A, Scenes 16 and 17).
[*Exit Soldier.*] [*J. Q. Adams.*]
12. *I'll shift:* I'll get along all right.
15. *Commodevales: comment allez-vous* (?). [*J. Q. Adams.*]

Scene Seventeen

2. *villiago:* villager (?). Cf. *2 Henry VI*, IV, 8, 48: "I see them lording it in London streets,/Crying 'Villiago!' unto all they meet."

15. *comparteve*. From *compartir*, to show compassion (?). [*J. Q. Adams.*]
18. *lamedst me in thy short ell*. Hopkinson, p. 51: "Derick means that the Frenchman lamed him with his short sword, which was a short ell, i.e., 27 in., in length." J. Q. Adams: "'To measure with a short ell' was a proverbial phrase meaning to deal unfairly."
22. *spilt:* killed.

Scene Eighteen

[*Another part of the battlefield.*] The events related in this scene and in Scene 20 actually took place on May 20 and June 3, 1420, at Troyes.
20. *it skills not:* it matters not.
21. *sit beside the saddle:* "To abandon oneself to despair?" (*N.E.D.*) [*J. Q. Adams.*]
54. *Kate.* See p. 103.
57. *canst thou tell how to love.* . . . Monaghan, pp. 356–57, notes several parallels between the language of the ensuing dialogue and that of *Henry V*, v, 2, 107 ff.
66. *abated.* J. Q. Adams' reading for "related" (both quartos).
86. *at host with:* in agreement with (?). Cf. p. 161.
93. *rouse:* shake.

Scene Nineteen

11. *Four or five times slain.* Cf. Falstaff's "eleven buckram men grown out of two!" (*1 Henry IV*, 11, 4, 243). [*Monaghan.*]
32. *reparel.* John's blunder for apparel.
40. *be hanged in thy own language.* Cf. "I can drink with any tinker in his own language" (*1 Henry IV*, 11, 4, 21). [*Monaghan.*]
65. *because we be soldiers.* Soldiers and apprentices assumed the liberty of setting fire to houses of ill-fame. [*J. Q. Adams.*]

Scene Twenty

8. *the late injuries offered me.* The King refers to his reception of the Herald in Scene 15; we have learned of the firing of the camp in Scene 16.
11. *for one:* as one who had a part in it.
20. [*Reads.*] [*J. Q. Adams.*]

*THE CASE FOR
SHAKESPEARE'S
AUTHORSHIP*

TESTS OF CHARACTER

Almost everyone who knows Shakespeare well agrees that his individuality is distinct. We should somehow be able to recognize as his any extensive piece of his writing yet unidentified. But there has never been any consensus as to what the tests of authenticity should be. Hardly anyone will argue that external data, if there were any, could induce us to believe that he wrote—say, *Tamburlaine* or *Volpone;* and few have ever doubted that one man created the canonical plays. The more reliable witnesses to Shakespeare's authorship of his work are, in fact, internal, though we have not adequately defined them. To do so, we should need to identify the idiosyncrasies of style which constitute his peculiar mode of expression, and as such are partly a matter of what he uniquely has to say, and partly a matter of how he uniquely says it.

It is beyond the scope of this undertaking to attempt to adduce more than a few of the criteria of Shakespeare's individual way of writing. To begin with, we shall consider certain aspects of his characterizations. It is true, to paraphrase

Coleridge, that we come to know Shakespeare's men and women much as we come to know people in "real life."[1] The acquainting process is the same, moreover, whether the plays are realized in the theater or in the reader's imagination. Of particular significance in this argument is the fact that Shakespeare's characters, like real people, only gradually manifest themselves. And, whereas almost everything said and done is meant ultimately to assist us in defining character, to the last we may often remain unsure, for the characters can always surprise us; their flexibility is perhaps the secret of their vitality, as in living men and women it is a source of personality.[2]

At first acquaintance, then, Shakespeare's characters are often quite imponderable. They may be self-confessed as unable to comprehend themselves and one another; they may speak in ignorance of their apparent motives. As observers, we guess at the causes and import of their vacillations; we come to know them as best we can. If real men and women fitfully elude and tantalize us, through Shakespeare's art we may be brought to know, though sometimes also we never quite know, his creations.

Prince Hal, in *1 Henry IV*, is just such an imponderable

---

[1] Coleridge, pp. 198–99: "The characters of the *dramatis personae*, like those in real life, are to be inferred by the reader;—they are not told to him. And it is well worth remarking that Shakespeare's characters, like those in real life, are very commonly misunderstood by different persons in different ways."

[2] I am aware that it is something like heresy nowadays to urge the verisimilitude of Shakespeare's characters. In an influential essay, L. C. Knights (p. 1) derides, as being only "the most fruitful of irrelevancies," the opinion that Shakespeare "was able to project himself into the minds of an infinite variety of men and women and present them 'real as life' before us."

character. And so is Prince Henry in *The Famous Victories*. As for Prince Hal, it may be observed that in his roistering days his father could not quite fathom him—nor could his associates. Very many critics have been troubled by an apparent disingenuousness and even incongruity in him and by deliberate ambiguities in relevant matters of fact. The soliloquy at the end of Act I, Scene 2, has been particularly vexatious, offering, it seems to some, an intolerable rationale of his present behavior and future intent. Hal promises that in due time he will be more princely, but the zest with which his words ask to be recited bespeaks his good spirits, if not frivolity. Saying in these confidences what he presumably thinks he might well say, and as he has the effrontery to say it, he displays no genuine remorse or any misgiving about himself.[3]

Moreover, Shakespeare leaves us uninformed as to whether the Prince was for long—or ever—engaged in robbery on the highways. The "once in my days I'll be a madcap" (1, 2, 159) suggests that we are to witness his first such venture; certainly he plays no direct part in the robbery. Although some have concluded that Hal has been only too much in love with this particular "sport," a hanging matter in Elizabethan England, they would be hard put to prove their opinion. The dramatist, I maintain, did not intend to be quite

---

[3] Although Miss Bradbrook, pp. 192–97, is quite unfair to Prince Henry (and *The Famous Victories*), she is right in saying that Prince Hal is, in fact, "reformed from the beginning. His notorious first soliloquy does not proclaim his intention of having his fling and repenting at leisure; it announces a policy of moral disguise." And Traversi, p. 6, asserts that, "Whatever his father may fear, Hal is never truly subjected to the vices with which he associates for ends he has deliberately, and with full consciousness, made his own." Cf. also Bailey and Ridley, cited in Evans, p. 8.

plain with us.[4] We finally like Hal the better for having had some doubts about him.

The chroniclers before Shakespeare were in disagreement about Prince Henry. Several believed that his youth had been irresponsibly misspent, but they, one and all, sought to glorify him as Hero King of England. Edward Hall, a chief source for the anonymous dramatist of *The Famous Victories* (and for Shakespeare), judged that he underwent a profound spiritual conversion, giving as an example Henry's "change of manners" by an act of sheer will.[5] Hall did not, in fact, know many details of Henry's youthful career.[6] He did not hesitate to affirm that it had been abandoned to "wanton pastime and riotous misorder." It is unlikely that he thought the Prince's "wavering vice" incipient virtue, though his phrase may have offered the anonymous playwright a clue. For him, the ultimate change was remarkable and possibly miraculous. Henry was "almost the Arabical Phoenix, and amongst his predecessors a very paragon."

It was John Stow (1580) who first gave currency to the narratives out of which the playwright of *The Famous Victories* contrived the robbery at Gad's Hill and the rioting in Eastcheap. Stow's version of the former event[7] was as follows:

---

[4] The Prince is apparently led to participate at Gad's Hill on the promise that he and Poins will be but witnesses of the robbery (1, 2, 189 ff.), although Poins has just sketched a quite different plan (180 ff.). It may be remarked in passing that, whatever Shakespeare's intention in *1 Henry IV*, his contemporaries were persuaded that Prince Hal had once been a highwayman; cf. the anonymous play, *Sir John Oldcastle*, iii, 3, *passim*. See also n. 10, below.

[5] *The Union of the Two Noble and Illustrious Families of Lancaster and York* (1550). See Hall, f. HV, i, *recto* (App. A, Scene 9).

[6] He was not familiar with the *Vita Henrici Quinti* (after 1437) of Titus Livius, or the translation of 1513; cf. Kingsford, pp. xv, xlvi.

[7] For the latter, see App. A, Scenes 2 and 3.

Whilst his [Prince Henry's] father lived, being accompanied with some of his young lords and gentlemen, he would wait in disguised array for his own receivers, and distress them of their money. And sometimes at such enterprises both he and his company were surely beaten. And when his receivers made to him their complaints, how they were robbed in their coming unto him, he would give them discharge of so much money as they had lost. And besides that they should not depart from him without great rewards for their trouble and vexation; especially they should be rewarded that had best resisted him and his company, and of whom he had received the greatest and most strokes. But after the decease of his father there was never any youth or wildness might have place in him, but all his acts were suddenly changed into gravity and discretion.

(Stow, pp. 582–83)

It will be seen that Stow does not, in fact, give an account of robbery at all.[8] To amuse himself and to try their mettle, he says, the Prince waylaid not the King's taxgatherers, as in *The Famous Victories* and, presumably, in *1 Henry IV*,[9] but his own. He displayed no finical misgivings about his conduct. On occasion he took a good blow for the fun of it. In the end he magnanimously overlooked his servants' losing their charge and returned their moneys. He was a sporting figure who acknowledged the dictates of *noblesse oblige*. The change which came over him as king was scarcely moral reformation. Whereas earlier he had been dashing and full of devices after the fashion of aristocratic youth, he at length began to take himself seriously.

Influenced by Hall, the playwright of *The Famous Vic-*

---

[8] Solly-Flood, p. 130, as historian, points out that *The Famous Victories* is "the very first work in which Prince Henry is said to have been engaged in any criminal enterprise whatever, or to have associated with thieves or buffoons."

[9] The Chamberlain describes the franklin who is to be robbed as "a kind of auditor" (II, 1, 63), and Bardolph announces, "There's money of the King's coming down the hill, 'tis going to the King's exchequer" (II, 2, 56–57).

tories presents the Prince's youthful character as irresponsible. His Henry impresses us, first off, as an unattractive swaggerer.[10] His associates are contemptible;[11] his participation in their winnings is criminal. An accomplice in the robbery of his father's receivers, he bullies them; he has no evident scruples about spending the booty. Stow's interpretation, however, significantly qualified the sketch. There is fleeting qualm of conscience or decency credited in Henry's request: "Tell me, sirs, think you not that it was a villainous part of me to rob my father's receivers?" (Scene 1, lines 9–10.) And he accepts Ned's reply, "It was but a trick of youth," only (and perhaps nervously) to change the subject. His lamed shoulders prove he has been no mere spectator in the fray, but he has left the act of theft to others—he has no prize to report for himself. To be considered, also, are his egalitarian sentiment ("We are all fellows" [88]), his disgust with his man Cutter's crassness ("Now base-minded rascal to rob a poor carrier!" [25]), and his fidelity even to this disreputable friend ("I'll save the base villain's life, if I may" [26]). Finally, for this scene, he tells us that he likes the "pretty wench" at the old tavern—just for her talk (Scene 1, lines 84–85); this would seem to show some measure of restraint in him. (The chroniclers are silent on this subject, and the item evidently stems from the playwright—a small point which, for its worth, helps to substantiate Shakespeare's authorship of *The Famous Victories;* as

---

[10] According to Miss Bradbrook, p. 193, "The Hal [*sic*] of *The Famous Victories* is a rowdy young prodigal, not differing at all from *The London Prodigal* or Mattheo of *The Honest Whore* or any of the roaring boys."

[11] By the stage directions, however, they are indicated as "Knights"; cf. Stow's "young lords and gentlemen" (see text above).

has often been remarked, he regularly prefers and advocates chastity in youth.[12])

From the start, Prince Henry is a complex and imaginative compilation. His ambiguity derives from the divergent interpretations of the sources. Full advantage is taken of their diversity. The materials are deliberately and adroitly reconciled. A new and original characterization results, quite worthy of Shakespeare and peculiar to his art. Henry is problematic and intrigues us to speculation. We may, indeed, resort to Shakespeare himself for diagnosis of the puzzling Prince in this phase of his development; speaking through Bolingbroke in *Richard II*, he indicates Henry's youthful complexity, declaring him to be:

> As dissolute as desperate, yet through both
> I see some sparks of better hope, which elder years
> May happily bring forth.
>
> (v, 3, 19–21)

Warned by solemn Hall, the author of *The Famous Victories* had not exculpated his brash young princeling. Though he presented him as wavering in his viciousness, he was but momently amiable. Stow had, in fact, justified Henry, and the playwright seems to have hinted he might sooner or later try to do so.

The "great debate" between the Prince's men and men of the Court when they were at supper in Eastcheap, which Stow mentions briefly [13] and Hall not at all, provided the resourceful dramatist of 1586 a sequel to his first episode, though he does not dramatize his materials except in narra-

---

[12] Miss Bradbrook, p. 195, observes of Prince Hal that he is not "given to women."

[13] See App. A, Scenes 2 and 3.

tive.[14] Disturbing the peace, he shows, has consequences even for a prince. Henry is haled to the Counter for riot. The King, it appears, later secured his release—we are not told how. We do not know whether the receivers retrieved their losses.[15]

A third writer contributed substantially to the development of the dramatic Prince Henry. This was Sir Thomas Elyot, who first cited the mutual "placability" of the Prince, King Henry IV, and the Chief Justice, as manifest in a memorable affair which took place at the Court of the King's Bench when the Judge refused to release one of the Prince's servants who had been arraigned for felony.[16] Scene 4 of *The Famous Victories* presents it. Elyot's interpretation of the whole situation (to the credit of everyone) had carried the persuasiveness of a not quite improbable possibility.[17] He evidently knew nothing of the tradition reported by Hall that the Prince, in a fit of insolence, "struck the Chief Justice with his fist on the face." [18] The playwright again sought to reconcile apparently incompatible materials; his intention cannot be understood without recourse to the sources. Thus, in deference to Elyot, he gives the King (in Scene 3) and the Judge (in Scene 4) various things to say to

---

[14] Scene 2, lines 97 ff.; see also pp. 110–11.

[15] In *1 Henry IV*, as in Stow's story, the Prince pays back the money, "with advantage"; cf. II, 4, 599 and III, 3, 200. In *The Famous Victories* the King presumably pays all; see pp. 114–15.

[16] *The Book of the Governor* (1531). See App. A, Scene 4.

[17] Solly-Flood, p. 55: "On examining Elyot's story of the Prince it will be found so extravagantly minute in its details as at once to suggest its origin to be due to the mere imagination of the writer, and that it was never intended by its author to be accepted otherwise than as a romance composed for the edification and amusement of his patron, Henry VIII."

[18] See App. A, Scene 4.

establish their equitableness; and Henry restrains Ned, who would decapitate the Judge for insubordination. Then, mindful of Hall, he has the Prince deliver the blow: a rather petulant "box on the ear." Next, however, Henry, to rid himself of his cronies (and at the same time perhaps indicating a moment's embarrassment), sends for musicians. He will now deal with the Judge alone, he says. But he is forthwith sentenced to prison, and *pace* Elyot, offers no more protest than: "Why, then, belike you mean to send me to the Fleet!" (101). The Prince does not oppose the officers who take him away. I should expect the reader unfamiliar with *The Book of the Governor* to miss the point, but the actor who understood the part—it was first played by William Knell [19]—could have indicated the playwright's meaning: that after his display of temper, the Prince resigned himself, accepting the penalty.

It is, of course, a fact that Shakespeare did not dramatize this scene in his later revision. Perhaps he thought it had failed in the old play, or did not wish to do something over in the same way. He had not forgotten it, we know, and could, no doubt, count on some in his audience to remember. Reference first occurs in Falstaff's attempted conciliation of the Judge:

For the box of the ear that the Prince gave you, he gave it like a rude prince, and you took it like a sensible lord. I have checked him for it, and the young lion repents—

(*2 Henry IV*, I, 2, 218-21)

Sir John takes credit for bringing Hal to his senses. He did not know, it seems, that the Prince had voluntarily submitted himself. Later on, however, Shakespeare has Hal

---

[19] See p. 180.

(now King) reassure the Judge, who is full of grim imag-
inings:

> And I do wish your honours may increase
> Till you do live to see a son of mine
> Offend you, and *obey you, as I did.*
> So shall I live to speak my father's words:
> "Happy am I, that have a man so bold
> That dares do justice on my proper son,
> And not less happy, having such a son,
> *That would deliver up his greatness so*
> *Into the hands of justice.*
> 　　　　　(*2 Henry IV*, v, 2, 104–12) [20]

If Henry's virtue of complaisance was not quite clear in
the old play, it becomes Hal's peculiar quality in *1 Henry
IV*.[21] It there accounts for his unresentful acceptance of his
father's stinging rebukes, for his fair estimate of Hotspur's
qualities, for his willingness to risk his life in single combat,
for his charitableness toward the dead enemy, for his cheerful surrender of any claim to honor after Hotspur's death,
and for his asking freedom for Douglas. These items do not
derive from the chronicles. This furbishing of the Prince's

---

[20] It will be noted that whereas "that" (109) refers to the Chief
Justice, "that" (111) refers to Prince Hal.

[21] According to Traversi, p. 5, "From the outset, the supreme quality inherited by Hal from his father and raised by his own practice
to new levels of shrewd calculation is *detachment:* a *detachment*
from traditional conceptions which he turns into the active intelli-
gence so firmly applied by him to his relatively legitimate situation,
but which is at the same time—and to forget this is to fail to respond
to the balanced conception of his character—his limitation as a human
being." Hal is, indeed, detached; he establishes his princeliness by
maintaining a certain distance between himself and his companions.
He is certainly not meanly calculating, as Traversi implies. His
placability is spontaneous; it accounts for both his charm and his
worth. Traversi, p. 165, is even wider the mark when he finds in Hal
"a controlled frigidity . . . unnaturally ascribed to youth."

character was, it seems to me, a fulfillment of what had been attempted in *The Famous Victories*. Shakespeare and the anonymous playwright, in fact, shared the same intention.

For the first half of the play, Henry's course of action is more checkered than is Hal's in *1 Henry IV*. While notice is given of his potential decency, the early episodes are generally raucous. At no point does he seem more reckless than in the little scene which just precedes his repudiation of his past (Scene 5). In it, as previously, the dramatist intends us to observe in Henry a calculated preposterousness. Ranging freely, the Prince gives Ned and Tom no inkling of his submission to the Judge ("Gog's wounds, Ned! didst thou not see what a box on the ear I took my Lord Chief Justice?" [1–3]). He is full of promises about the topsy-turvy regime he will establish at his father's death ("My lads, if the old King, my father, were dead, we would be all kings" [15–16]). The prisons will be turned into "fence-schools"; Ned will be Lord Chief Justice. He must now visit his ailing father, the Prince says, but allows none to suspect a moment's remorse ("I stand upon thorns till the crown be on my head" [50–51]).[22] He wears an extravagant garb—not, I think, a disguise;[23] it symbolizes his affectation and expresses his whim ("Cloak, eyelet-holes, needles, and all was of mine own devising; and therefore I will wear it" [46–47]). He professes himself determined to defy the good opinion of everyone at Court ("There's some will say the young Prince will be 'a well toward young man'— and all this gear, that I had as leave they would break my head

---

[22] The playwright presumably supposed such idle talk had been responsible for the rumor that the Prince intended to usurp the throne; see Stow (App. A, Scenes 5 and 6).

[23] See Explanatory Notes: Scene 6, line 8.

with a pot as to say any such thing" [54–57]).[24] He has reached the utmost pitch of his waywardness—but, on the evidence of what follows, he knows it.

The Prince and his friends cross over to the King's Palace. There is a brief ruckus with the Porter, ancestor, it may be guessed, of a stubborn breed in Shakespeare;[25] but, as in the previous scene, at Ned's offer of violence Henry's pretension fails ("Though I would help you in other places, yet I have nothing to do here. What! you are in my father's Court" [70–72]). It is evident once more that he is not to be taken at face; he has all the time been deliberately absurd. At a trumpet the King enters, accompanied by Exeter. Oxford presently announces the Prince's presence with a "very disordered company"; whereat the King anticipates an attempt upon his life. The Prince's claim that he has brought his knights to do his father "countenance" is too plainly specious to be mistaken as an effort at deception. The King will see none but his son, in the safekeeping of his courtiers. Prince Henry dismisses his cronies with a flourish.

The succeeding episode in the Inner Chamber is melodramatic, and Shakespeare will substitute for it the slowest-moving scene in *1 Henry IV* (iii, 2), intending, perhaps, to establish the (somewhat tedious) reasonableness he seems ultimately to admire in both the King and the Prince. Scene 6 is the anonymous playwright's attempt to represent the remarkable "change of manners." For this purpose he dramatizes the meeting in a "secret chamber," which had been

---

[24] In *2 Henry IV* (ii, 2, 60 ff.), the Prince expresses himself as disgusted with the cynicism of men in general; in *The Famous Victories*, he condemns their optimism.

[25] On the reputation of porters, cf. *Timon of Athens*, ii, 1, 10. See also *The Comedy of Errors*, iii, 1, and *Macbeth*, ii, 3.

reported by Stow.[26] The tearful King, noting the Prince's unsheathed dagger and stating his interpretation of the outrageous cloak, laments Henry's hardness of heart. Henry at once confesses his guilt in general terms, and kneeling before his father, offers him the dagger.[27] The gesture is artificial but nonetheless theatrically effective; it is, besides, a favorite device with Shakespeare.[28] We have been carefully prepared for the Prince's declaration of remorse. We see now that the cloak was worn that it might be disavowed and cast off as "ruffianly," along with the ruffian friends; the dagger was carried that it might be surrendered.[29]

The King is silent as his son kneels before him. With melancholy words the Prince rises to depart. After a moment his father calls back his self-styled "wild slave," [30] and, as he again kneels before him, pardons him. "No doubt but this day, even this day, I am born new again," says the penitent

---

[26] See App. A, Scenes 5 and 6.

[27] See App. A, Scene 1, n. 1.

[28] Similarly Cassius presents his dagger to Brutus in *Julius Caesar*, IV, 3, 100, and Imogen hers to Pisanio in *Cymbeline*, III, 4, 69; Richard proposes Anne avail herself of his sword in *Richard III*, I, 2, 175. Cf. also *True Tragedy of Richard III*, p. 8, line 10, and *King Leir*, p. 356, lines 5 ff.

[29] I must disagree with Miss Bradbrook's opinion (p. 194) that, "There is no hint that Hal [i.e., Prince Henry] ever had an earlier thought of repentance, indeed his language and manners make it impossible such should have been the intention."

[30] The "wildness" of the Prince is first mentioned by Hall, f. HV, i, *recto*. Shakespeare speaks of it frequently in *1* and *2 Henry IV*, and after the death of his father, the new King seems oddly to make him his scapegoat:

> My father is gone wild into his grave,
> For in his tomb lie my affections.
>
> (*2 Henry IV*, v, 2, 123–24)

Henry, paraphrasing Scripture and Hall.[31] From the start, even by his tautness, the playwright has indicated vacillation in Henry. Now and at last (though before witnesses he is histrionic, as royalty must ever be) the Prince is properly filial—if not altogether the "Arabical Phoenix." So understood, the portrait has its peculiar poignancy.

Scene 8 derives from Hall, who, because he dates the Prince's reformation after his coronation, has no concern to present his behavior in this episode sympathetically.[32] As it is managed in *The Famous Victories*, however, it seems intended to substantiate Stow's—and Elyot's—conception of the Prince. It begins with the King's exacting an oath of allegiance to his son from Exeter and Oxford. When the Prince enters, on his second visit to his sick father, his continuing remorse at his old neglect, his despair at having not yet craved pardon for all, his Job-like curse of the hour of his birth, his tears—all must be understood as sincere. There is a moment of doubtful import: that in which he takes the crown from his father's head as the latter sits in stupor. Hall had reported that the Prince removed the crown from a pillow on the King's bed. I can only think that the playwright's Prince acts without malice or stealth; he intends to relieve his father of the weight ("O my dying father!" [18–19]), or thinking him to be indeed dead ("Finding you at that time past all recovery, and dead, to my thinking" [46–47]), purposes to secure the crown for himself. Hall obviously had misgivings about the Prince's motives, and the dramatist, be it noted, allows the Prince no immediate word of explanation. I believe that, as in the crucial moment before the Judge, it is once again the actor's gesture that must

---

[31] See Explanatory Notes: Scene 6, line 45.
[32] See App. A, Scene 8.

give the audience the clue: sad and reverent, Henry should carry the crown in his hands, not wear it, as he exits.[33]

It is worthwhile to examine the scene that derives from this: Scene 5 of Act IV, *2 Henry IV*. In this play there has been no previous reconciliation with the King; he now assesses his son as if the action of *1 Henry IV* had not occurred.[34] The Prince's entering remarks to Clarence and Gloucester are callous. What he says thereafter at the bedside hardly reconciles us to the fact that he indeed crowns himself; he goes out wearing the crown on his head. When after his brief sleep the King wakens to find it gone, he unhesitatingly blames the Prince, speaking at length on the ingratitude of sons. In *The Famous Victories*, on the other hand, the King's first thought is that the Prince's enemies are responsible. And we are not encouraged to doubt Henry's grief at his father's supposed death. In *2 Henry IV*, Hal's tears off stage are reported. His words on returning suggest a decision, perhaps now first taken, to reform:

> . . . If I do feign,
> Oh, let me in my present wildness die,
> And never live to show the incredulous world
> The noble change that I have purposed!
>
> (IV, 5, 152–55)

In *The Famous Victories*, to be sure, the King suspects his son's defection ("Do you now begin again?" [41]) when he learns that it is he who has taken the crown, but straightway Henry's profession of innocence as he kneels weeping

---

[33] This seems to me the implication of Scene 8, lines 60–61: "It shall never touch my head so long as my father lives."

[34] The King is evidently unaware of the Prince's promised reformation (*1 Henry IV*, III, 2) and does not remember his achievement at Shrewsbury.

cancels question. Requiring him to stand, the King easily forgives him and conveys the crown into his hands with brief comment on the pain it has cost him.[35] The playwright's version of the Prince's reply somewhat softens the harsh words reported by Hall. The King is pleased with his son's assertion of his right to the succession. He predicts he "will be as warlike and victorious a prince as ever reigned in England" (72–73). Exeter and Oxford confirm him in the opinion. The King dies content.

The rest of the play belongs to the New Man, who, if sometimes bumptious, is now consistent in purpose, quickly decisive, energetic for England. Even before his coronation, he has demanded the crown of France, and immediately thereafter he prepares his invasion. Ned, Tom, and Jockey briefly interrupt him as he leaves the Abbey, but they are peremptorily rejected.[36] Ned is advised to mend his manners, for Henry's "unfeigned grief" for his father will not be eased by "flattering and dissembling" talk. Tom is banished from the royal presence. Jockey, alias Sir John Oldcastle, is passed over in silence. Surely no one will ask that the King should have wasted more time on these fellows.

It is interesting to compare what then follows (Scene 9) with the opening scenes of *Henry V*. The playwright of *The Famous Victories* had mainly been eager to simplify

---

[35] Perhaps the first mention of regret, though not guilt, on the part of Henry IV appears in Stow (1592), p. 545. Of Thomas of Clarence he says to Prince Henry, "I fear that he through his high mind will make some enterprise against thee, intending to usurp upon thee, which I know thy stomach may not abide easily. And for dread hereof, as oft as it is in my remembrance, I sore repent me that ever I charged myself with the crown of this realm."

[36] Hall (f. HV, i, *recto*) and Stow (pp. 583–84) are not in exact agreement about the new King's treatment of his former associates; see App. A, Scene 9.

and hasten the chronicled materials. The Archbishop of Canterbury presents Henry's claim succinctly and advises: "You must take your sword in hand and conquer the right" (65). He goes on to advocate the prior invasion of Scotland, usurping the arguments of Westmorland in Hall.[37] Oxford (instead of Exeter in Hall)[38] would "conquer France and conquer both." The later expansion of all this in *Henry V* is a puzzling complication. There, the intrigue of the churchmen and the over-long and sophistical defense of Henry's right to the French throne, with its grotesque comment on the Salic law, in effect jeopardize the legitimacy of the English cause. Devious ecclesiastical policy recommends war. Doughty traitors call into serious question Henry's right to the English crown itself. Seemingly, it is the Dauphin's taunt that fixes Henry's determination to subdue France.

In the later play, the character of the King is, in fact, conceived with scant reference to the Prince Hal of *1 Henry IV*. We may wonder whether we must not question Shakespeare's art as well as his success.[39] There is no such problem in *The Famous Victories*. The Prince Henry of the first half of the play could not in changing have become other than the strident figure of the second. We should note, however, that Scene 9 ends with new evidence of the placability that Elyot claimed for the man. The anonymous dramatist, hav-

---

[37] See f. HV, iii, *verso–x, verso* in App. A, Scene 9; see also Facts and Inferences, n. 92.

[38] *Loc. cit.*; see also Facts and Inferences, n. 72.

[39] As has been shown by Tillyard and others, Shakespeare attempted to integrate several of his history plays into trilogies (and even tetralogies). Originally, however, he conceived most of these plays as separate entities and did not intend them for performance in sequence; nor did he write them in the order of their events. The difficulties raised by the attempt to interpret them in their interrelationships have been underestimated in recent criticism.

ing read in Hall that, in place of former flatterers, Henry "elected and chose men of gravity, men of wit, and men of high policy, by whose wise counsel and prudent instruction he might at all times rule to his honor and govern to his profit" (f. HV, i, *verso*), determined to exemplify this point in his treatment of the Lord Chief Justice. Thus, Henry appoints him Protector of the realm for the duration of the wars in France,[40] and the King regards this action as "the chiefest thing of all" (155–56). Shakespeare repeats the episode in *2 Henry IV*, v, 2.

In the rest of the play, however, there are no further touches of this kind. Neither is there any real inconsistency with the character previously established. Henry becomes in turn the fearless warrior, the fierce and somewhat vindictive victor, the peremptory peacemaker, the blunt wooer. His rhetoric before and after the battle lacks the exhilarating brilliance of Shakespeare's later rant, but it has sufficient resonance. In his condescending banter with the coy Princess Katherine, he offers precedent to Petruchio and Hotspur in their chatter with their Kates.[41] And we suppose he talked to the pretty wench at the old tavern in Eastcheap in the same vein.

We have now surveyed the career of the Prince in the old play, comparing Shakespeare's later treatment of the same materials. We have found in the earlier version a para-

---

[40] But see Hall, f. HV, xi, *recto*, in App. A, Scene 9, and App. B, Item XIII.

[41] Shakespeare's ladies of this name tend to be shrewish—and attractive. Hotspur teases his wife affectionately when he nicknames her Kate. The sailor's song of drunken Stephano (*The Tempest*, ii, 2, 51) is a minority report: "But none of us cared for Kate./For she had a tongue with a tang. . . ." Was the tradition inaugurated by Kate Tarlton? Cf. *Tarlton's Jests*, p. 17, *et passim*.

doxical complexity in Prince Henry (with concomitant mystification of the audience) and emergent self-command, the presentation of a positive virtue—complaisance and placability, the maintenance of over-all consistency. We have come to know this Henry gradually, as we come to know a man in real life—and in Shakespeare. We have found him full of surprises for us, alive and fully engaged in the flux of things, yet himself throughout. It is an achievement in characterization of which no writer known to have been at work in 1586, other than Shakespeare himself, can have been capable.

Shakespeare learned much from this exercise. The imponderability of his Prince Hal is quite comparable, though it is handled less mechanically. Ambiguities in motivation and in matter of fact serve much the same purpose in the later characterization; we must wonder before we find assurance. Shakespeare sets himself the same assignment, though he changes the interpretation, for reasons to which we shall return in the next chapter.

We have seen that both plays can be better understood in the light of their sources. The anonymous playwright was greatly influenced by Edward Hall; his text proves this. If it was he who wrote the annotations in Alan Keen's copy of *The Union of the Two Noble Houses . . . of Lancaster and York* (see App. B), his interest in Hall's political philosophy was already aroused. These early concerns became preoccupations of Shakespeare as long as he undertook the dramatization of English history.[42]

It was almost certainly owing to Hall that the playwright of *The Famous Victories* created a Prince Henry who, though he began by outraging ordinary decencies, reformed

---

[42] Cf. Tillyard, *passim.*

at last. But he was fully aware that Stow saw Henry as having been consistently a prince. And Elyot, dismissed by Hall, had testified strongly in Henry's behalf. The playwright, pondering these interpretations, discovered his task: to transcend the chronicles by reconciling in fiction their various reports.[43] Shakespeare, a decade later, cannot simply have imitated the anonymous writer's procedure; rather, I maintain, he returned to an earlier undertaking with which he had come to be dissatisfied. And his final solution of the riddle of Hal's nature, after he had elsewhere exploited and perhaps wearied of Hall, shows him utilizing the previous experiment, achieving fuller correspondence with Stow and Elyot, creating a play much the same, very different, and far greater.

2 Henry IV and *Henry V* are sorry sequels to *1 Henry IV*. I am inclined to believe that they are somewhat earlier works hastily reorganized, with additions, to serve as sequels. No one will gainsay that *1 Henry IV* is, in any case, the real and culminating achievement of the lot. It is in that play that Hal emerges as perhaps the most ingratiating character in Shakespeare. He could hardly have made him what he is, if he had not undertaken the earlier experiment. *The Famous Victories* is the first essay—not a failure, properly read, yet for all that somewhat clumsy.

Before leaving this section of my study I should like to recapitulate four bits of minor evidence for Shakespearean

---

[43] Only Hopkinson, pp. xi–xii, seems hitherto to have recognized the ingenuity of the characterization: "The portraiture of Prince Henry, as Prince and King, although wanting in distinctness, shows considerable subtilty and skill deserving of praise."

authorship which, if at this stage in our argument they can be dismissed as coincidental, must ultimately be reckoned with numerous other such items as proof:

1) The characteristically Shakespearean item of Prince Henry's restraint in matters of sex. The youthful protagonist in Shakespeare, if he is ultimately to be idealized, must retain his chastity.

2) The stubborn porter. A moment's humor, doubtless not first employed here, but to become part of Shakespeare's stock in trade.

3) The dagger offered as proof of remorse and willingness to submit oneself wholly to another's whim. This item— also, it may be, not original here—becomes a favorite device with Shakespeare.

4) The bandying with a shrewish Kate. The Prince talks to his Kate as, it appears, Shakespeare supposed high-spirited youths must talk to ladies of this name.

Some attention must be given to comic characterization in *The Famous Victories*. To Thomas Rymer and, after him, to Dr. Johnson, comedy was the characteristic expression of Shakespeare's genius,[44] and to very many, his comedy has seemed unique. Our problem of identification is complicated by the fact that as long as Richard Tarlton lived, his taste must have influenced the style of the Queen's, the company which first staged *The Famous Victories*.[45] The comedian may, or may not, have given the

---

[44] Rymer, p. 169; Johnson, p. 100.
[45] For the evidence that Tarlton played the part of Derick, see pp. 176, 180–81.

playwright general or detailed suggestions concerning his part. The play must have offered full scope to Tarlton's techniques and talents, but it was not written merely as his vehicle or just for comedy's sake. Moreover, the laughter is not confined to the scenes dominated by the Clown, and there is separate and abundant fun aplenty.

Falstaff's spirit is by anticipation present in the Clown. Professor Stoll long ago observed that Shakespeare "was acquainted with the play, and drew from it the traits of Falstaff's cowardice, thievishness, and loose living, the touches of repentance and sanctimoniousness, and his friendship with Hal."[46] But the hulk Sir John and Derick are far from equal. Moreover, it should be pointed out that some of the traits of Falstaff are found not in the Buffoon but in Prince Henry. Thus in Scene 1 the Prince voices Falstaff's notion of how young men must live. His hesitations are about as serious as the qualms "Monsieur Remorse" will feel.[47] His agility in avoiding the embarrassing subject is Falstaff's.[48] He also tries to "fear" men with words.[49] His humor, like Falstaff's, is perverse, and indulged at any cost. His gusto is great, Sir John's overwhelming. We hear Falstaff's idiom in Henry's "Bravely spoken, lads!" "as I am a true gentleman, I will have the half of this spent to-night!" and "we are all fellows. I tell you, sirs, if the King my father

---

[46] Stoll, p. 75. Monaghan, p. 358, elaborates the point: "A superficial examination of the two plays will show that in each we have a swaggering soldier, in service against his will, aggressive when his enemies are unarmed and running away when they are armed; in each he is a coward, braggart, glutton, thief, rogue, clown and parasite; in each he has the same monumental, unblushing effrontery and loves a jest even at his own expense."

[47] Cf. *1 Henry IV*, I, 2, 125.

[48] Cf. *1 Henry IV*, I, 2, 44.

[49] Cf. *1 Henry IV*, II, 2, 87 ff.

were dead, we would be all kings." When, in Scene 5, the Prince sketches a gloriously licentious future without prisons or penalties for men of daring, his imagination achieves Falstaffian range.[50] The Receivers themselves, in their attempt to implicate the Prince and his cronies in the robbery, use the Falstaffian manner of insinuation; note, for example, their insistence upon such incriminating details as number, color, and size.[51]

But Derick, if he is only a partial realization of Falstaff, is the ultimate center of attention in every scene in which he appears.[52] The stage is quiet for the raucous hue and cry of his first entrance (in Scene 2). The midnight confusion, his frantic resistance to the Watch with dagger drawn, his pretentious refusal to be arrested, his fellow-feeling for the other three "poor men," his forgiveness of everybody—all these must have been quite delicious in competent hands. John Cobbler momently warns of a passenger's approach: it is Cutbert Cutter, the Prince's "setter" of "matches," common thief.[53] Derick, intending him as his quarry, forever nicknames him "Gad's Hill" from the place of their encounter.[54] "Gad's Hill" is somehow overpowered and dragged off to Newgate.

On the evidence of this scene alone, Falstaff's debt to Derick is plain. Consider, for example, Derick's mock gentility ("Zounds, masters, do clowns go in silk apparel? I am sure all we gentlemen-clowns in Kent scant go so well"

---

[50] See pp. 121–22.

[51] Cf. *1 Henry IV*, ii, 4, 206 ff.

[52] He is not allowed to compete directly with the Prince, but he wins the one exchange of words they have; cf. Scene 4, lines 60–61.

[53] Cf. *1 Henry IV*, i, 2, 119; ii, 2, 53.

[54] Shakespeare retains only the nickname in *1 Henry IV*.

[36–38]).[55] He boasts of his self-restraint and displays the magnanimity of the supercilious: "Nay, I am quickly pacified. . . . 'Tis a wonderful thing to see how glad the knave is, now I have forgiven him." (55–61).[56] Shakespearean in manner, if not exclusively Falstaffian, are Derick's ready repartee (*Thief.* Zounds! I am one of the King's liege people. . . . / *Derick.* Marry, sir, I say you are one of the King's filching people [78–84].[57]) and irony ("I'll be very charitable to thee, for I will never leave thee—till I see thee on the gallows" [125–26] [58]).

Derick, like Falstaff, loves a "play extempore."[59] Thus, in Scene 4, after the Judge has accepted Henry's box on the ear and sent him to the Fleet, there ensues the amusing take-off in which Derick, persuading John to assume the Judge's chair, runs over with him the preceding scene. So captured by the illusion is John that he thinks he has actually condemned Derick to prison and sits melancholy and bemused as Derick goes out (148 ff.). We remember the enrapt Falstaff, playing Hal, who would "play out the play" though the Sheriff and a hue and cry are at the door.[60] Falstaff would not break the illusion; John cannot. Both have suspended disbelief.

Derick, like Falstaff, is a gourmand, pretending to deny it: "I am none of these great slouching fellows that devour these great pieces of beef and brews. Alas, a trifle serves me—a woodcock, a chicken, a capon's leg, or any such little

---

[55] Cf. *1 Henry IV*, III, 3, 92.
[56] *Ibid.*, III, 3, 192. Cf. p. 139.
[57] Cf. *Henry V*, III, 2, 48.
[58] Cf. the ironic use of "charitable" in *Titus Andronicus*, II, 3, 178; III, 2, 70; IV, 2, 43.
[59] Cf. *1 Henry IV*, II, 4, 309.
[60] Cf. *1 Henry IV*, II, 4, 531 ff.

thing serves me" (158–61).[61] Both terrify with resounding and fatuous accusations; compare Derick's "She is a very knave, and thou a drab if thou take her part" (Scene 7, lines 14–15) with Falstaff's "Go to, you are a woman, go" (*1 Henry IV*, III, 3, 70).

Scene 10, in which Derick, John, and Cutbert Cutter are pressed into the King's service is particularly to be noted. The farewell of John and his wife is as mawkish, if not as maudlin, as Falstaff's departure from Tearsheet.[62] Derick's relations with Mistress Cobbler are not more peaceable than Falstaff's with Dame Quickly.[63] In short, the scene is Shakespearean—and witty—in itself, and the cause of wit in other scenes.[64]

On the battlefield (Scenes 17 and 19), Derick's combination of cowardliness, candor, evasion, resourcefulness, wit, and bravado is, in little, Sir John's formula at Shrewsbury and Gaultree. He rushes on pursued by a Frenchman who spares his life on the promise of "tre, four hundred crowns." Derick's one condition is that he shall lay them on the Frenchman's sword. This granted, the sword gets into Derick's hands, he hurls the Frenchman down, exults triumphantly over him. In terror, the victim runs away. Says Derick, "Mass, I am glad of it. For, if he had stayed, I was afraid he would have stirred again, and then I should have

---

[61] On Falstaff as glutton, cf. Wilson (1944), pp. 25 ff.

[62] *2 Henry IV*, II, 4.

[63] Monaghan, p. 357: "Derick, it seems, lives with John, the cobbler, drinks his ale, 'eats him out of doors' and quarrels with his wife, while Falstaff takes his ease in his inn, quarrels with his hostess, and 'eats [but especially drinks] her out of house and home,' as he puts 'all her substance into that fat belly of his.' "

[64] Cf. *1 Henry IV*, III, 3; *2 Henry IV*, III, 2; *Henry V*, II, 1 and 3.

been spilt. But I will away to kill more Frenchmen" (Scene 17, lines 20–23). John Cobbler is evidently as great a coward as he: "I scaped hardly; for I was within half a mile when one was killed!" (Scene 19, lines 5–6). And Derick confesses: "Every day when I went into the field I would take a straw and thrust it into my nose and make my nose bleed; and then I would go into the field" (Scene 19, lines 16–19).[65] He is proud of his own absurdity; consider his tale of a fight with another Frenchman (Scene 19, lines 21–27).[66]

As a comic type, Derick is not really the Braggart Soldier; he is scarcely akin to Parolles and but distantly to Pistol. Yet he is no ordinary Buffoon. He is presumably Tarltonian—but obviously Shakespearean. Not yet Falstaff, he supplies important factors of that great product.[67]

One might almost argue the Shakespearean authorship of *The Famous Victories* on the basis of the painstaking and loving attention afforded minor characters. Some evidence of this has already been presented, but we should particularly consider the opening of Scene 2, in Billingsgate Ward, near Eastcheap, at midnight. What occurs there lingers, if only subconsciously, in Shakespeare's mind as he contrives

---

[65] Stoll, *loc. cit.*, notes of Falstaff that, "like the cowardly Derick of *The Famous Victories of Henry V*, he had persuaded them all to tickle their noses with speargrass, and to hack their swords with their daggers." Cf. *1 Henry IV*, ii, 4, 335 ff.

[66] Cf. *1 Henry IV*, ii, 4, 216.

[67] Monaghan, pp. 360–61: "What we know . . . is that Shakespeare found the prototype of Falstaff in the well-marked characteristics of Derick, the clown, that he grafted these on Sir John Oldcastle, and that they grew, under his magic hand, and developed into the greatest jester of all time, the immortal Falstaff."

long afterwards the immortal Watch of *Much Ado*.[68] Here is neither Dogberry nor Verges "to present the Prince's own person," [69] but neighbors John Cobbler, Robin Pewterer, and Lawrence Costermonger are as unpretentious "good men and true" [70] as ever Hugh Otecake and George and Francis Seacole will be. After assigning Robin to Pudding Lane End, Lawrence and John chatter of the "toward young Prince" who, they agree, is "one of these taking fellows"; the King may well end by disinheriting him. They are, like Dogberry, "loath to have anything ado" (51); they subside and fall asleep. At this point in the play we may also notice "any ado" (*bis*: 8, 9), and "such ado" (27–28); "much ado" itself occurs in line 108 and in Scene 3, line 32. The language of the Watch in *Much Ado* repeatedly echoes *The Famous Victories*. Thus Dogberry's "we are the poor Duke's officers" (*Much Ado*, III, 5, 22) recalls Derick's reference to the Constable's "*bad* officers" (Scene 2, line 47).[71] The testimony of the Second Watchman: "I know that Deformed . . . 'a goes up and down like a gentleman" (*Much Ado*, III, 3, 133–35) seems reminiscent of Derick's "Zounds, masters, do clowns go in silk apparel? I am sure all we gentlemen-clowns in Kent scant go so well"

---

[68] It is instructive to study two other instances of similar foolery on the same theme and of about the same date as *The Famous Victories*, in Lyly's *Endymion*, IV, 2, and the anonymous *King Leir*, v, 3 and 5. Though not without wit, both lack comic characterization.

[69] Cf. pp. 128–29.

[70] Compare Lawrence's suspicion of "Gad's Hill" ("We know thee not to be a true man," Scene 2, line 77) with Dogberry's "If you meet a thief, you may suspect him, by virtue of your office, to be no true man" (*Much Ado*, III, 3, 52–53). And note Dogberry's leading question: "Are you good men and true?" (*loc. cit.*, line 1).

[71] Note also Elbow's phrase: "I am the poor Duke's constable" (*Measure for Measure*, II, 1, 48).

(Scene 2, lines 36–38). And "I be but a poor man" (*Much Ado*, III, 5, 30), though it is a common locution, repeats Derick's "You seem to be poor men" (Scene 2, lines 54–55). Must we not conclude that in the later play Shakespeare deliberately imitated this scene, that he derived its title from it, and, finally, that he in fact revised his own materials?

Those inclined to judge *The Famous Victories* as hack writing would do well to compare the Boy's picturesque account of the affair at the old tavern in Eastcheap (end of Scene 2) with the Mayor's dignified recapitulation. The Boy gives a breathless narrative of the Prince's arrival with "three or four more of his companions"; he had heard them call for "wine good store" [72] and a "noise of musicians"; [73] he well knows they were "very merry for the space of an hour," though his sense of time is vague. All of a sudden, he says, "our pots flew against the walls," and a "bloody fray" [74] broke out in the street. The Boy may be supposed to have watched what happened thereafter from safe vantage; but the events were too confused for him to attempt a report. The Mayor, at the outset, depends on what he has heard from others, including, we judge, the Boy. He summarizes what is reported to have happened before his arrival. Thus he mentions only the approximate time of the outbreak, avoids committing himself as to the exact number of the Prince's company, describes them simply (and moderately) as "very disordered." He has been told of the futile efforts of the watchmen (no more stalwart, perhaps, than John Cobbler and his men). He and the Sheriff with diffi-

---

[72] "Good store" is idiomatic; cf. *2 Henry IV*, IV, 3, 131; *Coriolanus*, I, 9, 32.

[73] See Explanatory Notes: Scene 2, lines 99–100.

[74] The phrase is common in Shakespeare; see p. 155.

culty stopped the brawling, he says. Afterwards, they considered their duty carefully. The King's loving subjects who
dwelt at hand had been greatly disquieted. It might just be,
the officials guessed from the presence of the Prince, that the
King was testing them in the matter. They therefore, to
prove their fitness for their responsibilities, committed him
to the Counter, but the King might be assured that his son's
every need was being considered.

The Boy's tale and the Mayor's report are thus wholly
in character. They are constructed by a writer gifted with
empathic feeling and imagination—such as Shakespeare's.

THE PRINCE AS MASK

A theef of venisoun, that hath forlaft
His likerousnesse, and al his olde craft,
Can kepe a forest best of any man.
CHAUCER, The Physician's Tale (83–85)

John Keats was thinking of Shakespeare when he declared that "A Poet is the most unpoetical of any thing in
existence, because he has no Identity—he is continually informing and filling some other body." [1] As a generaliza-
tion, the statement is a half-truth, tempting but absurd in
relation to Shakespeare or to Keats himself. There can be
no question that any poet commonly imparts much of himself to all his creations. Keats elsewhere noted this of Shakespeare, saying that he "led a life of Allegory; his works are
the comment on it." [2] The statement implies that Shakespeare regarded his personal experience as in some measure
representative; his figments are an attempt to communicate
it symbolically, and they prove his detachment from it.

In particular, a writer's early work often reflects his personal experience, and the details of his biography, if they can
be recovered, will assist us in understanding his writings. In
the case of Shakespeare the data are sparse. And we do not

---

[1] Keats, p. 228, with Beaumont's emendation.
[2] *Ibid.*, p. 305.

know whether to credit some of the stories which have been reported. Some continue to doubt, for example, whether we should accept the statement of Nicholas Rowe, writing almost a century after his death, that Shakespeare left Stratford because he had been prosecuted for poaching by Sir Thomas Lucy. Here is the familiar account:

He had by a misfortune common enough to young fellows, fallen into ill company; and amongst them some that made a frequent practice of deer stealing, engaged him with them more than once in robbing a park that belonged to Sir Thomas Lucy of Charlecote, near Stratford. For this he was prosecuted by that gentleman, as he thought, somewhat too severely; and in order to revenge that ill-usage, he made a ballad upon him. And though this, probably the first essay of his poetry, be lost, yet it is said to have been so very bitter that it redoubled the prosecution against him to that degree, that he was obliged to leave his business and family in Warwickshire, for some time, and shelter himself in London.[3]

That Rowe's narrative is plausible is the opinion of so cautious a scholar as E. K. Chambers, who has given an able analysis of the supporting evidence.[4] I do not know, however, that anyone has hitherto suggested that Shakespeare's intense interest in Prince Hal in *1 Henry IV* may have derived from the fact that he himself had once been guilty of ill-considered complicity in robbery. Such an experience no doubt had ultimately to be rationalized—with accounting given—by so sensitive a conscience as such a man probably possessed. It seems to me quite possible that Shakespeare's exoneration of Hal as never having been actually contami-

---

[3] Cf. Chambers (1930), II, 265. What is perhaps a fabrication of the ballad is discussed by Adams (1923), p. 89. Rowe also remarks that in *The Merry Wives of Windsor* Shakespeare made Falstaff "a deer-stealer that he might at the same time remember his Warwickshire prosecutor under the name of Justice Shallow."

[4] Chambers (1930), I, 18–21.

nated by the selfishness and greed of thieving, notwithstanding appearances, may have had its model in his mental struggle to exculpate himself in his own eyes. And whoever accepts the likelihood of this must be prepared to face the question whether *The Famous Victories*, which handles very similar materials, is not another (and earlier) version of the same poet's defense, not only of the Prince but of himself. On this level of their meaning, the two plays are, I believe, variant apologies for the affair at Charlecote, whether recognized as such by Shakespeare's contemporaries or not.

We must remember that although Sir Thomas Lucy and the law presumably saw as robbery pure and simple the escapade of Shakespeare and his cronies (Ned, Tom, and Jockey?), the future playwright may have counted himself responsible only for disturbing the baronet's peace. Poaching of this kind was a common enough recreation among young blades of the time.[5] More seriously on his conscience may have been his affront to his father's dignity. According to Rowe, he soon left Stratford—under some sort of duress. Perhaps, however, it was such an act of complaisance as Henry and Hal might have been capable of. It appears that he presently sought from afar to vindicate himself.

The Prince of *The Famous Victories* is at the outset a giddy swasher, and in 1586 this may have been Shakespeare's estimate of himself as he had been at home, at his worst. But his Henry is endowed with a fitful decency, though he cannot steadily command himself. Ultimately, he makes things right with his father. Since in *The Famous Victories* it is

---

[5] Cf. Adams (1923), p. 81. Halliwell-Phillips (1843), p. 105, adducing the diary of Dr. Simon Forman, a contemporary of Shakespeare, remarks that, "If a bishop could steal deer when he was at college, surely Shakespeare could do so in his early career without his respectability being impeached by his editors."

presumably the King, not the Prince, who foots the bill, one may guess that it was John Shakespeare who restored Sir Thomas' losses. Ten years afterwards, on the other hand, to judge from *1 Henry IV*, Shakespeare seems to have felt less defensive; he may have begun to regard his youth, as do men in general, nostalgically. His Hal could claim to have been misunderstood, for he had never been more than a somewhat too cheerful and uncritical spectator of crime on the highways. Like the earlier Henry, he greatly disappointed his father but set things aright. And, like Stow's Prince, he paid back the money.

Support to my interpretation is afforded by the crucial paragraph in Stow, characterizing the youthful Henry.[6] It has been pointed out by others in discussion of Rowe's story that the plays themselves prove that Shakespeare knew much about hunting.[7] In that case, what thoughts must have passed through his mind when he first read Stow's statement that the Prince "was of marvelous great strength, and passing swift in running, insomuch that he with two other of his lords without bow or other engine, would take a wild buck or doe in a large park"? Surely this was a feat for any huntsman to admire, whether equalled at Charlecote or elsewhere.

And there follows Stow's inapposite remark concerning the Prince, which would certainly have caught Shakespeare's attention: "He delighted in songs and musical instruments, insomuch that in his chapel amongst other his private papers, he used certain Psalms of David translated into heroical English meter by John Lydgate, Monk of Bury." It will be remembered that the anonymous dramatist

---

[6] See App. A, Scene 1.
[7] Butler, p. 47.

finds occasion frequently to mention Prince Henry's liking for music;[8] it was another interest, I venture, he shared with his protagonist.

After these matters, Stow comes to the story of how Henry with his young lords and gentlemen held up the receivers on the highways and "distressed" them of their moneys *for the fun of it*. In reading this, I say, Shakespeare must have recognized the Prince for another self. It may at once have occurred to him to use Henry as a sort of psychological correlative in a play. As he sought to set forth the Prince's motives and action, he must almost inevitably have assessed his own.

The father-son relationship is an obvious and important theme in both *The Famous Victories* and the derivative plays. In the tradition of the Prodigal's Return, it is, according to Wilson and others,[9] the unifying principle of *1* and *2 Henry IV*. Hall and Holinshed agree that, after he had suppressed civil dissension in his realm, Henry Bolingbroke was much loved by the nobility for his gentleness.[10] Elyot celebrated in him, as we have seen, the virtue of placability.[11] And in *The Famous Victories* kindly traits are noted in his character. He gives no hint of earlier wrongdoing.[12] But whereas in the chronicles the last illness is simply diagnosed as apoplexy,[13] the Prince's behavior is here made in some degree responsible for his father's sickness. From the start, the Prince commits deliberate outrage against him: he robs

---

[8] See Scene 2, lines 99 ff.; also 3, 24–25; 4, 88; 5, 106–7.

[9] Wilson (1944), *passim*. But cf. Goddard, p. 161.

[10] See Hall, f. HIV, xxxii (App. A, Scenes 5 and 6); cf. Holinshed, p. 1163a.

[11] See App. A, Scene 4.

[12] See Tests of Character, n. 35.

[13] For example, Hall (see App. A, Scenes 5 and 6).

the King's receivers at Gad's Hill, not his own, as in Stow. He gleefully anticipates his father's death, manifesting no hint of affection for him: "if the King my father were dead, we would be all kings" (Scene 1, lines 89–90). The King at his first appearance is lamenting that he has gotten him "a son which with grief will end his father's days!" (Scene 3, lines 45–46). After the second imprisonment, the King's grief is touched with something of the pathos of complaisant David's lament for Absalom: "Oh, my son! my son!" (Scene 5, lines 81–82). Later on, the Prince's vindication of himself and his reconciliation with his father coincide, but it is the Prince's remorse at his mistreatment of his father that chiefly motivates his change of heart.

We know a good deal about Shakespeare's father.[14] By calling he was a glover, whittawer, and perhaps butcher. He became a man of position in Stratford, holding a variety of municipal offices, including Justice of the Peace, High Bailiff, and Chief Alderman. As of 1580, however, his fortunes had begun to fail. About this time, according to Rowe, he withdrew his son William from the Free School because of the "narrowness of his circumstances and the want of his assistance at home."[15] And in that year, it is a matter of record that he incurred heavy fines for failure to provide surety for good behavior.[16] He thereafter became negligent in his attendance at the meetings of the Stratford Corporation, although he remained an alderman until 1587. In 1592 he is listed in the recusancy returns for Stratford for ab-

[14] Cf. Chambers (1930), I, 11 ff.
[15] Cf. Chambers (1930), II, 264.
[16] Chambers (1930), I, 15. Smart, pp. 66–73, argues that the charges had resulted from his recusancy as a Papist and failure to attend the services of the Church of England.

sence from church, with a notation: "fear of process of debt." [17]

Throughout there is, in fact, no imputation against the character of John Shakespeare. In all probability he was generally respected and liked. In his prosperity, we know, he was generous with others.[18] He is described, late in life, as "a merry-cheekt old man," who said of his son, "Will was a good honest fellow," but, we are told, "he dares have crackt a jest with him at any time." [19] It is likely that there was a warm bond of affection between son and father, and it may well have been a matter of shame to both of them when Sir Thomas Lucy, once the recipient of official hospitality from John Shakespeare, started public proceedings against William for poaching. The young man, no doubt already concerned for his father's welfare, must have felt that he had now added to his embarrassment publicly. Recompense was in order. He went to London. It is my opinion that in writing *The Famous Victories* he intended a kind of apology for his shortcomings. When the Queen's Players were in Stratford in 1587,[20] they may well have performed *The Famous Victories* at the playwright's instance, as a guarantee to the citizenry of his now mature responsibility. John Shakespeare, one hopes, held thereafter his head high

It is, moreover, virtually certain that William Shakespeare restored his father's fortunes when prosperity came to him a decade later. In 1596 application was made at the College of Heralds in John Shakespeare's name for the granting of

---

[17] Smart, p. 72.
[18] Adams, p. 24.
[19] *Ibid.*, p. 34.
[20] Chambers (1923), II, 107.

a coat of arms, in renewal of a request dated twenty years
earlier.[21] In 1597 the poet was able to purchase New Place,
the most pretentious mansion in Stratford.[22] John Shakespeare, when he died in 1601, must have been satisfied with
the return of his prodigal son to respectability. Henry Monmouth's precedent, we may suppose, had been often in the
playwright's mind.

---

[21] Adams (1923), p. 284.
[22] *Ibid.*, p. 252.

THE LANGUAGE

The testimony of the language of *The Famous Victories* must now be considered. Others have remarked that words and phrases from the old play are repeated by Shakespeare in *1* and *2 Henry IV* and in *Henry V*,[1] but the extent of his indebtedness, which in fact manifests itself also in many plays of the canon besides these three, has never been shown. The processes of association at work have not been investigated, and the significance of the relationship has not been assessed.

It is difficult to decide upon the proper criteria in analysis. I think, for example, that the last thirty lines of Scene 4 in the play are peculiarly Shakespearean. The dialogue of Derick and John is that farrago of quaint wit, lovable stupidity, innocent absurdity, whimsy, and pathos which Shakespeare often affords.[2] Derick, petty fraud that he is,

---

[1] Thus, Greer (June, 1954), p. 240, cites eighteen instances of similarity, concluding that "No two authors working independently could have arrived at so much similar phraseology."

[2] Superior examples: Launcelot and his poor father, William and Audrey, Launce and his dog, Dogberry and the Watch.

leads John by the nose. Miserable John, his gull, aglow with good fellowship, sings a ditty as redolent of Elizabethan England as the anonymous "Back and Side Go Bare" and "The Nut-brown Ale." Might not the poet of Winter's Song in *Love's Labor's Lost* (v, 2) himself have composed John's lesser verses? If any agree with me that only Shakespeare can have written the whole passage, I may take it that impressionistic judgment can be shared; it is not just fancy. But I find no solid evidence on which to rest my case.

Apart from John's verses and a couplet here and there, the language of *The Famous Victories* is prose. Nevertheless, its rhythms and the gusto of its rhetoric sometimes approach poetic tension. In this respect it is, of course, like Shakespearean prose generally. Consider this piece of extravagance:

Prince. But, Ned, so soon as I am King, the first thing I will do shall be to put my Lord Chief Justice out of office, and thou shalt be my Lord Chief Justice of England.

Ned. Shall I be Lord Chief Justice? By Gog's wounds, I'll be the bravest Lord Chief Justice that ever was in England!

Prince. Then, Ned, I'll turn all these prisons into fence-schools, and I will endue thee with them, with lands to maintain them withal. Then I will have a bout with my Lord Chief Justice. Thou shalt hang none but pick-purses, and horse-stealers, and such base-minded villains; but that fellow that will stand by the highway side courageously with his sword and buckler and take a purse—that fellow, give him my commendations! Beside that, send him to me, and I will give him an annual pension out of my exchequer to maintain him all the days of his life.

(Scene 5, lines 19–34)

The encomium of "that fellow," in its repetitive phrases and rhythms, recalls the Fat Knight's apologia (*1 Henry IV*, II, 4, 522–27). And it will be noted that the Prince's transvaluation of values approximates Falstaff's. Moreover, one is reminded quite specifically of a passage in the derivative play:

> *Falstaff.* . . . Do not thou, when thou art king, hang a thief.
> *Prince.* No, thou shalt.
> *Falstaff.* Shall I? Oh, rare! By the Lord, I'll be a brave judge.
> *Prince.* Thou judgest false already. I mean thou shalt have the hanging of the thieves and so become a rare hangman.
>
> (I, 2, 69–76)

In the later trilogy there are, indeed, innumerable instances of such clearly deliberate imitation and borrowing of language and ideas; they do not by themselves provide proof of unity of authorship. Less intentional, perhaps, is the repetition of patterns of rhythm, but here the data are fitful, and general similarities certify nothing.

Definite aural resemblances I take to be more significant. Thus, in the passages cited, Ned's "Shall I be Lord Chief Justice? By Gog's wounds, I'll be the bravest Lord Chief Justice that ever was in England!" is to be set beside Falstaff's "*Shall I? Oh*, rare! *By* the *Lord*, *I'll be* a *brave judge*." In addition to the italicized items, which are almost exact equivalents, there are interesting alterations: the repetition of "Lord" in the first passage seems to induce the substitution of "By the Lord" for "By Gog's wounds" in the second; "the bravest Lord Chief Justice" is modified to "a brave judge"—perhaps because the Chief Justice does not figure in *1 Henry IV*. Such concern with the sound and quality of language, involving alterations in small details, suggests scrupulous revision, motivated, I infer, by the special responsibilities of proprietorship.

I. Still more persuasive, because the echoes are found not in the derivative trilogy but in other plays of the Shakespearean canon, is the sort of evidence provided by Prince Henry's phrase, artful in its alliteration, assonance, and consonance: "*pick-pur*ses and h*orse-s*teal*ers*," [3] which may be compared with the following passage from *Hamlet:*

> *Rosencrantz.* My lord, you once did love me.
> *Hamlet.* So I do still, by these *pickers and stealers*.[4]
>
> (III, 2, 348–49)

G. L. Kittredge, following Whalley, has noted that in Shakespeare's day the catechism of the Church of England advised the catechumen to "keep his hands from 'picking' and 'stealing.'" [5] The key words probably enjoyed conjoint currency. It is safe to assume, therefore, that "pick-purses and horse-stealers" and "pickers and stealers" both echo the familiar language of the catechism. But "pickers and stealers" seems also indebted to the phrase from *The Famous Victories*, for the assonance of *ers . . . ers* is reminiscent of the consonance of *ers . . . ors . . . ers* in the earlier play.

Closer to the language of *The Famous Victories* is Celia's sardonic praise of Orlando as lover, in *As You Like It:* "I think he is not a pickpurse nor a horse-stealer" (III, 4, 24).

No other examples of similar treatment of the words from the catechism are known to me. I conclude that one man's

---

[3] *Alliteration:* repetition of a consonant (often initial) in two or more words; e.g., repetition of *p*, *r*, and *s*, above.

Assonance: repetition of stressed vowel sounds; e.g., *u* in *purse*, *e* in *ers*, above.

Consonance: harmonious sequence of contrasting groups of sounds; e.g., *urs . . . ors . . . ers*, above.

[4] I am indebted to Professor John S. Weld, of Harpur College, for suggesting this passage.

[5] Kittredge, p. 231.

fancy was operative in all three instances. It is unlikely that Shakespeare would purloin such an item from *The Famous Victories* and modify it for use in *Hamlet* and *As You Like It* if it were not already his own. Even if he did not have the phrase from the old play consciously in mind when he wrote the related passages, unconscious processes of association could have been at work. And that this is the more likely can be shown by pointing out similarities in the contexts. Prince Henry's chatter with Ned and Tom occurs prior to his serious conversation with his father in the Inner Chamber, and Hamlet speaks frivolously to Rosencrantz and Guildenstern as he proceeds to a solemn interview with his mother in her closet. To Shakespeare, the awkward Orlando may perhaps have been reminiscent of the awkward suitor of Princess Katherine.

If the processes of association in these relationships were not conscious, the probability of imitation and borrowing is, of course, the less. Yet the meticulousness of the alterations itself seems significant. For, whereas the "picking" and "stealing" of the catechism had been marked by a repeated trochee and by the assonance of *ing*, the author of *The Famous Victories* introduced dactyls with alliteration and consonance. The phrase in *Hamlet* returns to the trochees of the catechism, with a difference—a new assonance. In *As You Like It*, the repetition of the phrase from *The Famous Victories* is almost identical.

The curious history of "pick-purses and horse-stealers" displays, then, its derivation from the catechism, Shakespeare's familiarity with the original and with the phrase in *The Famous Victories*, his close attention to the aural qualities of both, and his reworking of both. And in the later contexts there may well be associations with *The Famous Victories*. The very fact that the manipulations involve small matters is itself significant; such minor alterations, whether conscious in fact or the product of subconscious motives,[6] explain themselves most naturally if we assume unity of authorship. It is certain that, consciously or unconsciously, we treasure our merest verbalisms; and that in this Shakespeare was no different from the rest of us.

II. Hardly less significant is the handling of a passage from Edward Hall by the anonymous author and by Shakespeare. In describing King Henry's celebrated maneuver at the Battle of Agincourt, Hall wrote:

> . . . to the intent to vanquish the power of the French horsemen which might break the order and array of his archers . . . he caused stakes bound with iron sharp at both ends of the length of 5 or 6 feet, to be pitched before the archers and on every side of the footmen like an hedge . . .
>
> (f. HV, xvi, *verso*)

It will be remembered that in *The Famous Victories* Henry orders the lines of battle at Agincourt as follows:

> . . . I will that every *archer* provide him a *stake* of a tree, and *sharpen* it at both ends; and, at the first encounter of the *horsemen*, to *pitch* their *stakes* down into the ground *before* them . . .
>
> (Scene 14, lines 24–27)

Shakespeare may be shown to have used *both* of these passages in *1 Henry VI*. In the opening scene in Westminster Abbey (the funeral of Henry V), a Messenger reports from France that Talbot has been overthrown and

---

[6] Evidently the subconscious mind may borrow from itself. In proffering suggestions to the conscious mind it may or may not make known their origin.

captured as he withdrew from the siege of Orleans. The chronicles offered no basis for the statement that:

> He wanted pikes to set *before* his *archers*,
> Instead whereof *sharp stakes* plucked out of *hedges*
> They *pitched* in the *ground* confusedly
> To keep the *horsemen* off from *breaking* in.
>
> (I, I, 116–19)

That this passage derives—at least in part—from Hall rather than *The Famous Victories* is certified by the words *hedges* and *breaking;* on the other hand, that it derives also from *The Famous Victories* is suggested by the word *ground*. The author, or authors, of *The Famous Victories* and *I Henry VI* used the same passage from Hall; furthermore, with the exception of *hedges*, they borrowed the same words from Hall. And, finally, the author of *I Henry VI* borrowed the word *ground* from *The Famous Victories*.

The evidence, it appears to me, allows no other plausible explanation than that one man, Shakespeare, was at work.

III. Shakespeare long cherished Derick's complaint against Cutbert Cutter at the Court of the King's Bench:

. . . he hath not [only] beaten and wounded me also, but he hath beaten and wounded my pack, and hath taken the great raze of ginger that Bouncing Bess with the jolly buttocks should have had.

(Scene 4, lines 28–31)

First off, Derick's "*great raze* of *ginger*" is echoed by "*a gammon* of *bacon* and two *razes of ginger*" [7] in *I Henry*

---

[7] In passages from *The Famous Victories* italicization is intended to indicate internal aural relationships; in passages from the canonical plays it indicates both internal aural relationships and echoes from the parallel passage in *The Famous Victories*.

IV, ii, 1, 26. The new phrasing repeats the first in its last three words; it is also related by alliteration and assonance. Thus, the hard *g* of "*gammon*" echoes the *g* of "*great*"; the schwa vowel (ə) of the sequence *a . . . on . . . of . . . on . . . of* develops from "*of*"; *a* of "b*a*con" replaces *ea* in "gr*ea*t."

Futhermore, there is a significant relationship between the passage of *The Famous Victories* and one from *A Midsummer Night's Dream* in which jealous Titania complains of Oberon that he would not be in Athens:

> But that, forsooth, the bouncing Amazon,
> Your buskined mistress and your warrior love,
> To Theseus must be wedded, and you come
> To give their bed joy and prosperity.
>
> (ii, 1, 70–73)

It was a far cry from Bess to Hippolyta, but that both ladies "bounced" was sufficient to animate a series of echoes. The sequence "*Beaten . . . but . . . beaten . . . bouncing . . . Bess . . . jolly buttocks*" becomes "*but . . . bouncing . . . buskined mistress . . . bed joy.*" Alliteration, assonance, and consonance are found in the first; variants and new relationships in the second. A metathesis, or transposition of sound, occurs between *cks* and *sk*. "B*ess*" and "mistr*ess*" are related by assonance. "*Jolly*" is intensified to "*joy.*" The whole constitutes one of the most complicated aural relationships I have discovered.

IV. A passage from *The Famous Victories* is approximated in *The Comedy of Errors*. Prince Henry's recommendation of "the old tavern in Eastcheap" had been as follows:

... there is good wine:—besides, there is a pretty wench that can talk well . . .

> (Scene 1, lines 84–85)

And there is similar praise of the accommodations at the Porpentine from Antipholus of Ephesus:

> I know a wench of excellent discourse,
> Pretty and witty, wild, and yet, too, gentle.
> There will we dine.
>> (*Comedy of Errors*, III, 1, 109–11)

The original passage had not, at a glance, been notable, yet from it Shakespeare repeated ideas and words in cluster, with similar phrasal patterns. "A pretty wench that can talk well" equates "a wench of excellent discourse, pretty and witty." The alliteration in "*wine* . . . *w*ench . . . *w*ell" recurs in "*wench* . . . *w*itty . . . *w*ild . . . *w*ill"; and the consonance is retained, with modification. "There is good wine" agrees rhythmically and in assonance with "There will we dine," and the emphatic usage of "there" is identical.

Circumstantial similarity in the two contexts is clear: Prince Henry and Antipholus profess comparable tastes. Shakespeare, writing for Antipholus, somehow bethought him of Henry and recast the language of the earlier play for the similar situation.

V. Although the plays of the derivative trilogy present innumerable instances of rewriting the text of *The Famous Victories*, in many of these no conclusion as to unity of authorship is warranted. Consider, however, such a pair of passages as:

. . . in striking me in this place you greatly abuse me; and not me
only but also your father, whose lively person here in this place I do
represent.

(Scene 4, lines 95–98)

> I then did use the person of your father . . .
> Your highness pleased to forget my place . . .
> The image of the King whom I presented,
> And struck me in my very seat of judgement.
>
> (*2 Henry IV*, v, 2, 73–80)

Here the two contexts are related: in the first the Judge
upbraids the Prince; in the second he defends his own conduct. The borrowing was certainly conscious and deliberate.

Obvious parallelisms are these:

> striking me—struck me
> place—place
> abuse—use
> your father—your father
> lively person—image
> person—person
> in this place—in my very seat of justice
> I do represent—I presented

There is, moreover, a treasuring of sounds. The alliteration, assonance, consonance, and metathesis exemplified in
the sequence "*place . . . person . . . place . . . represent*"
are preserved with a difference in "*person . . . pleased . . .
place . . . presented.*"

Shakespeare, in writing the second of the passages, clearly
had an ear for, as well as an eye on, the first. We may assume
that as he recalled the earlier passage its aural ingenuities
challenged him. Would he have accepted that challenge if
he had not had a proprietary interest in them? Was it not
that he was Shakespeare and they were his?

Compare also with the foregoing Macbeth's:

> Here had we now our country's honour roofed
> Were the graced *person* of our Banquo *present* . . .
>   (III, 4, 40–41)

And note, incidentally, that Dogberry's "You, Constable, are to *present* the Prince's own *person*" (*Much Ado*, III, 3, 79) recalls the same text in parody, as does Quince's "say he comes to disfigure, or to *present*, the *person* of moonshine" (*A Midsummer Night's Dream*, III, 1, 62).

VI. In Scene 10 occurs the impressment of Derick, John, and the Thief into the King's service. "Gad's" is just out of jail, and Derick frets about his probable filching of shirts.[8] When Shakespeare phrased Falstaff's protests about his conscripts:

> I'll not march through Coventry with them, *that's flat*. . . . I had the most of them *out of prison*. There's but a *shirt* and a half in all my company . . . and the shirt, to say the truth, stolen . . .
>   (*1 Henry IV*, IV, 2, 42–49)

he must have remembered the disreputables of Scene 10. I have italicized "that's flat" because it echoes Scene 10, line 33, and the repetition of this unpretentious bit of slang certifies the relationship.

---

[8] Cutbert Cutter would presumably have satisfied Captain Falstaff's requirements for a good infantryman: "Where shall I find one that can steal well? Oh for a fine thief, of the age of two and twenty or thereabouts!" (*1 Henry IV*, III, 3, 210–12).

VII. A curious development occurs from King Henry's rationalization: "If we cannot have it [i.e., food] for money, we will have it by dint of sword; the Law of Arms allows no less." (Scene 12, lines 10–12) "Dint of sword" may be a cliché of the time;[9] it is worth noting, however, that it is elaborated by Shakespeare, with internal alliteration, metathesis, and consonance, in "by *indict*me*nt* and by *dint of sword*" (*2 Henry IV*, IV, 1, 128). Three words of the passage are associated again in *Richard III* (v, 3, 311): "Our strong *arms* be our conscience, *swords* our *law*." King Richard, the speaker, has just ordered his battle at Bosworth, in the manner of Henry the Fifth at Agincourt.

VIII. *Ri*g*ht* . . . *wrong* are proverbial opposites,[10] with alliteration and consonance. In *The Famous Victories* the phrase "*wrong*ful u*surp*ers of m*y right*" (Scene 12, lines 27–28) is an elaboration which adds assonance and metathesis. Shakespeare develops this further in "*t*hou u*surp'st my* fa*ther's right* and *m*ine" (*3 Henry VI*, v, 5, 37) and in "*t*heir *rui*n *that usurped our right*" (*ibid.*, v, 6, 73).

IX. "*All the* . . . in/of *the* w*orl*d" is not, I think, a common Elizabethan locution, but it is a favorite with Shakespeare, probably for the fixed rhythmical pattern, the alliteration,

---

[9] Holinshed (p. 1181a) uses it. It reappears in *The True Tragedy of Richard III*, p. 64, line 2, and as "dint of rapier" in *Friar Bacon and Friar Bungay*, Scene 10, line 85. Cf. also "dint of pity" in *Julius Caesar*, III, 2, 198.

[10] Tilley, p. 571.

and the curious (and inexact) consonance of *all . . . orl.*
It tends to induce other aural effects in context. It is significant for this argument that it appears, with attendant alliteration, in *The Famous Victories* in the King's remark
(Scene 8, line 2): ". . . *all the* physicians in *the* world
cannot cure me."

There are three examples from the canonical plays in
which the context closely resembles that of the passage
cited: Prince Hal's "*all the poison*ous *potions* in *the* world"
(*1 Henry IV*, v, 4, 56); Iago's intricate "*Not poppy, nor
mandragora,/Nor all the drowsy syrups* of *the world,/
Shall ever medicine thee* to *that sweet sleep . . ."* (*Othello*,
III, 3, 331–32); and Laertes' "*No* medicine *in the* world can
do *thee* good,/*In thee there* is *not* half *an* hour of life"
(*Hamlet*, v, 2, 325–26).

The following should also be compared:

> *Captain.* What! *Will* you fly, and *leave* Lord Talbot?
> *Fastolfe.* Aye! *All the* Talbots in *the* world, to save my life.
> *Captain.* Cowardly knight! *Ill* fortune follow *thee!*
> (*1 Henry VI*, III, 2, 107–9)

> *Eleanor.* What seest thou there? King Henry's diadem,
>   Enchased with *all the* honors of *the* world?
>   If so, *gaze on,* and grovel *on thy* face . . .
> (*2 Henry VI*, I, 2, 7–9)

> *Coriolanus.* . . . of *all the* men i' *the* world
>   I *would* have 'voided *thee* . . .
> (*Coriolanus*, IV, 5, 87)

And for a variant:

> *Caesar.* *We* could not *stall* together
>   In *the* whole world. But yet *let* me lament . . .
> (*Antony and Cleopatra*, v, 1, 39–40)

X. The *all* . . . wh*ole* consonance is also found in *The Famous Victories* and in many of the canonical plays, with and without an intervening *the:*

> *all* my wh*ole* army
> > (*The Famous Victories,* Scene 11, line 47)
>
> *all* the wh*ole* army
> > (*1 Henry VI*, I, 1, 126)
>
> *all* the wh*ole* inheritance
> > (*1 Henry VI*, III, 1, 163)
>
> make *all* wh*ole*
> > (*1 Henry IV*, II, 1, 81)
>
> *all* our joints are wh*ole*
> > (*1 Henry IV*, IV, 1, 83)
>
> *all* our wh*ole* city
> > (*Romeo and Juliet*, IV, 2, 32)
>
> *all* the wh*ole* synod
> > (*Antony and Cleopatra*, III, 10, 5)
>
> *all* the wh*ole* time
> > (*Henry VIII*, I, 1, 12)

XI. A sequence which made an impression on Derick and John—and, it seems, on its author—was: "Why, *I* pray *you*, my lord, who am *I*? . . . therefore to teach *you* what prerogatives . . ." (Scene 4, lines 92–98). This turns up again, elicited by Oswald's egregious insubordination, in *King Lear*, I, 4, 85–100:

> *Lear* (to Oswald). *Who am I*, sir? . . .
> *Kent* (to Oswald). *I'll teach you* differences.

XII. In Scenes 13 and 17, the conversation of the French soldiers attempts the comedy of substandard syntax and pro-

nunciation exhibited by foreigners.[11] In *Henry V*, without
precedent, to be sure, from Prince Henry's Kate in *The
Famous Victories*, the French Princess Katherine and her
attendant, Lady Alice, badly botch their English. In *The
Merry Wives of Windsor*, there is also the grotesque blun-
dering of Dr. Caius, the French physician. It is worth pointing out that the broken English of the ladies and Dr. Caius
is quite similar in its linguistic perversities to that of the
French soldiers in *The Famous Victories:*

1. *Me* used as the subject of verbs:

> *The Famous Victories*
> me will (Scene 13, lines 2, 13, etc.)
> me ha (Scene 13, lines 8, 14, etc.)
> me have (Scene 13, line 24)
> shall me tell? (Scene 13, line 28)
>
> *Henry V*
> me understand (v, 2, 136)
>
> *The Merry Wives of Windsor*
> me vill cut his ears (ii, 3, 66)
> me vill have it (ii, 3, 72)
> me vill kill de priest (ii, 3, 86)
> me have stay (ii, 3, 36)
> me tank you (ii, 3, 75)
> me dank you (ii, 3, 94)

2. *Mans* used as the plural of *man:*

> *The Famous Victories*
> the English-mans (Scene 13, lines 7, 10, etc.)
>
> *Henry V*
> de tongues of de *mans* (v, 2, 122)

---

[11] It anticipates the dialectal gibberish of Fluellen, Macmorris, and
Jamy in *Henry V.*

3. *T* for *th:*

> *The Famous Victories*
> tro: *th*row (Scene 13, lines 2, 5, 24)
> tre: *th*ree (Scene 17, line 6)
>
> *The Merry Wives of Windsor*
> tank: *th*ank (II, 3, 75)
> troat: *th*roat (I, 4, 114)

4. *Sh* for *ch:*

> *The Famous Victories*
> *sh*est: *ch*est (Scene 13, line 12)
> *sh*ildren: *ch*ildren (Scene 13, line 14)
>
> *The Merry Wives of Windsor*
> mu*sh*: mu*ch* (III, 2, 66)

Shakespeare's Frenchman's English is more elaborately and steadily maintained in the later plays than in *The Famous Victories*, but the similarities are striking.

XIII. Miscellaneous figures of speech and phrasing that occur in *The Famous Victories* are later favored by Shakespeare.

The pun, for instance, is adroitly handled. Note, in Scene 10, lines 3–18, the perversity of wit in the play on *go* (eight times in sixteen lines). And note Derick's "I'll *clap the law* on your back" (33), from the odd word "clapper-claw" to claw with one's nails.[12]

---

[12] Shakespeare plays with the word in *The Merry Wives of Windsor*, II, 3, 67–70:

> *Hostess.* He will clapper-claw thee tightly, bully.
> *Caius.* Clapper-de-claw! Vat is dat?
> *Hostess.* That is, he will make thee amends.
> *Caius.* By gar, me do look he shall clapper-de-claw me. . . .

And cf. the Address ("A Never Writer to an Ever Reader") in

An amusing example of climactic ordering is afforded by John's "Why, man, I cannot get a capon once a year—except it be at Christmas, at some other man's house" (Scene 4, lines 162–63). Professor Kittredge used to illustrate the figure by Kent's definition of Oswald: "the son and heir of a mongrel bitch" (*King Lear*, II, 2, 24).

Chiastic inversion is illustrated by Derick's "bring the bar to the prisoner" (Scene 4, lines 2–3) after the Justice's "bring the prisoner to the bar." Compare the Clown's reasoning in *Hamlet*, V, 1, 16–20: "If the man go to this water and drown himself . . . but if the water come to him and drown him . . ."

Lastly, the Prince's "case me no casings!" (Scene 4, line 80) exemplifies a depreciative and ironical rejection of a word—a device occasionally used by Shakespeare, but not peculiar to him. Compare "Grace me no grace, nor uncle me no uncle" (*Richard II*, II, 3, 85–87) and "Thank me no thankings, nor proud me no prouds" (*Romeo and Juliet*, III, 5, 153).[13]

XIV. The vocabulary of *The Famous Victories* includes few words unexampled in the later plays.[14] Certain oddities have significance in this argument since they are echoed later. Thus, *seal emanuel* (Scene 9, lines 142, 148), more properly *seal manual* (cf. *Venus and Adonis*, 516), is im-

---

Troilus and Cressida (Quarto of 1609): ". . . a new play, never stal'd with the stage, never clapper-clawed with the palms of the vulgar."

[13] Cf. also *True Tragedy of Richard III*, p. 63, line 23.

[14] Perhaps unique coinages are *Worenday* (Scene 4, line 151) and *flaunching* (Scene 13, line 43).

plicit, with the same humorous implications, in *2 Henry VI*,
IV, 2, 105–7:

> *Cade.* What is thy name?
> *Clerk.* Emmanuel.
> *Dick.* They use to write it on the top of letters. 'Twill go hard
> with you.

Villiago (Scene 17, line 2), probably a slang word,[15] is
also found in *2 Henry VI*, IV, 8, 48: "I see them lording it in
London streets,/Crying 'Villiago!' unto all they meet."

Some ordinary words, moreover, are used in what I take
to be Shakespeare's individual way. *Tables*, for instance,
often signifies with him the record of memory:

> I will write him in my *tables;* for so soon as I am made Lord
> Chief Justice I will put him out of his office.
> (*The Famous Victories*, Scene 5, lines 73–75)

> Who art the *table* wherein all my thoughts
> Are visibly charactered . . .
> (*Two Gentlemen of Verona*, II, 7, 3)

> And wide unclasp the *tables* of their thoughts . . .
> (*Troilus and Cressida*, IV, 5, 60)

> Yea, from the *table* of my memory . . .
> (*Hamlet*, I, 5, 98)

> My *tables*—meet it is I set it down . . .
> (*Hamlet*, I, 5, 107)

> Thy beauty's form in *table* of my heart.
> (*Sonnet XXIV*, 2)

And *Sonnet CXXII* elaborately plays on the word.

---

15 Cf. also *Everyman Out of His Humor*, V, 3, 68.

Odd in their ramifications are the echoes in Shakespeare of certain phrases from Exeter's speech in Hall (f. HV, vii, *verso*), advocating attack upon the French rather than upon the Scots. If the English assault their "poor neighbors" to the North, Exeter asserts, they will prove themselves "men effeminate, more meet for a *carpet* [i.e., for the dance] than a *camp*." The anonymous author transfers the *carpet . . . camp* phrase to the Dauphin's taunt of King Henry as reported by the Archbishop of Bourges: "you are more fitter for a tennis court than a field, and more fitter for a *carpet* than the *camp*" (Scene 9, lines 132–33). The insulting implication, though not the alliterative language, is retained by Shakespeare in a similar context, where the French Ambassador warns the English King: " . . . there's naught in France/That can be with a nimble galliard won" (*Henry V*, I, 2, 251–52). And perhaps in Bolingbroke's regretful remarks (*Richard II*, v, 3, 10) about that "young wanton and *effeminate* boy," the youthful Henry Monmouth, there is lingering reminiscence of Hall's language. We may also compare Sir Toby's description of Sir Andrew as a "knight, dubbed with unhatched [i.e., unhacked] rapier and on *carpet* consideration" (*Twelfth Night*, III, 4, 257–58).

XV. As we have seen, the pairing of commonly related concepts is often emphasized aurally by repetitive devices, such as alliteration and assonance, and by contrasting devices with a degree of sameness, such as metathesis and consonance. Ingenuity of this sort may have general appeal and acceptance —such expressions acquire currency and may even become hackneyed. In the speech of any individual, idiosyncrasies of taste account for the frequent recurrence of similar peculiarities.

A large number of paired words, frequently with reinforcing aural features, can be cited from the canonical plays; many of these are also found in *The Famous Victories*. Some of them belong to the common idiom of the eighties and nineties, but others I believe to be Shakespearean.

CLASS ONE

Paired words believed to be specifically Shakespearean.

1. pick-*purses* . . . ho*rse-steal*ers (related concepts, alliteration, assonance, consonance)

   [See Item I, above.]

2. *bon*fires . . . *ban*quets (related concepts, alliteration, consonance)

   > the French making of *bonfires*, and at their *banquets*
   > (*The Famous Victories*, Scene 14, lines 35–36)

   > make *bonfires*
   > And feast and *banquet* in the open streets
   > (*1 Henry VI*, 1, 6, 12–13)

3. *I* am pacified . . . *I* forgive (related concepts, alliteration)

   > Nay, *I am* quickly *pacified* . . . now *I* have *forgiven* him
   > (*The Famous Victories*, Scene 2, lines 55–61)

   > Hos*tess*, *I forgive thee*. . . . *Thou seest I am pacified*
   > (*1 Henry IV*, III, 3, 192–95)

4. kn*a*ve . . . dr*a*b (related concepts, consonance)

   > she is a very *knave*, and thou a *drab*
   > (*The Famous Victories*, Scene 7, lines 14–15)

Follow the *knave,* and take this *drab* away
                    (*2 Henry VI*, ɪɪ, ɪ, ɪ56)

If your Worship will take order for the *drabs* and the *knaves*
                    (*Measure for Measure*, ɪɪ, ɪ, 245)

5. *no*t *ki*ng . . . *nothing* (similar concepts, alliteration, assonance, consonance)

What! *not King* of France? Then *nothing.*
                    (*The Famous Victories*, Scene 20, lines 6–7)

I am *unking*ed by Bolingbroke,
And straight am *nothing*
                    (*Richard II*, v, 5, 37–38)

6. dr*u*nk . . . bl*oo*d (related concepts, assonance)

our swords are almost *drunk* with French *blood*
                    (*The Famous Victories*, Scene 15, lines 1–2)

Thy b*rother's blood th*e *thirsty earth* hat*h drunk*
                    (*3 Henry VI*, ɪɪ, 3, 15)

England's *lawful* earth,
Un*lawfu*lly made *drunk* with innocents' *blood*
                    (*Richard III*, ɪv, 4, 29–30)

7. *d*— . . . *d*umps (alliteration)

How *do* you *do* . . . put away these *dumps*
                    (*The Famous Victories*, Scene 9, lines 36–38)

to step out of these *d*reary *dumps*
                    (*Titus Andronicus*, ɪ, ɪ, 391)

Tune a *d*eploring *dump*
                    (*Two Gentlemen of Verona*, ɪɪɪ, 2, 85)

Why, how now, *D*aughter Katherine! In your *dumps?*
                    (*The Taming of the Shrew*, ɪɪ, ɪ, 286)

Oh, play *me* some *merry dump,* to comfort *me.* . . . Not a
dump we
>   (*Romeo and Juliet,* IV, 5, 108)

When *griping grief* the heart *d*oth wound
And *d*oleful *dumps* the mind oppress
>   (*Romeo and Juliet,* IV, 5, 128–29)

*Sing no mo*re *d*itties, *sing no mo*e
Of *dumps so d*ull and heavy
>   (*Much Ado,* II, 3, 72–73)

8. *scr——* . . . *scr——* (alliteration)

> *scr*ape and *scr*awl
>>   (*The Famous Victories,* Scene 8, line 35)

> *Scr*atch thee but with a pin and there remains
> Some *scar* of it.
>>   (*As You Like It,* III, 5, 21)

> *Scr*atches with briers,
> *Scar*s to move laughter only.
>>   (*Coriolanus,* III, 3, 51)

> What, art thou hurt? . . . aye, a *scr*atch, a *scr*atch
>>   (*Romeo and Juliet,* III, 1, 95–96)

> *scr*ip and *scr*ippage
>>   (*As You Like It,* III, 2, 171)

9. *valiant* . . . *v——* (alliteration)

> a *valiant v*ictory
>>   (*The Famous Victories,* Scene 14, line 13)

> of noble birth,
> *V*aliant and *v*irtuous
>>   (*1 Henry VI,* IV, 1, 34–35)

> a breathing *valiant* man
> Of an invincible, unconquered spirit
>
> > (*1 Henry VI*, iv, 2, 31)

> a Roman by a Roman
> *Valiant*ly *v*anquished
>
> > (*Antony and Cleopatra*, iv, 15, 57–58)

10. *wild . . . h——*

> young and *wild-h*eaded
> > (*The Famous Victories*, Scene 11, line 11)

> *T*am*i*ng my *wild h*eart to thy lovi*n*g *h*and
> > (*Much Ado*, iii, 1, 112)

> These *h*igh *wild h*ills
> > (*Richard II*, ii, 3, 4)

> *those that* tame *wild h*orses
> Pace 'em no*t* in *t*heir *h*ands
> > (*Henry VIII*, v, 3, 21)

> *W*ere in *wild h*urry
> > (*Coriolanus*, iv, 6, 4)

11. *feed . . . f——* (alliteration)

> in the *f*ield to *feed* crows
> > (*The Famous Victories*, Scene 14, lines 47–48)

[This is a favorite alliterative combination in Shakespeare. Bartlett cites 30 instances in the plays, 8 in the sonnets.]

12. *viled/villainous . . . youth*

> this *viled* and reprobate company, which abuseth *youth*
> > (*The Famous Victories*, Scene 6, lines 3–4)

> That *villainous* abominable misleader of *youth*
> > (*1 Henry IV*, ii, 4, 508)

CLASS TWO

Paired words noticed only in the canonical plays and in
The Famous Victories, *but supposed to have more general
currency.*

1. ruin . . . decay (similar concepts)

> it goes to *ruin* and *decay*
> > (*The Famous Victories*, Scene 5, lines 84–85)

> Cry woe, destruction, *ruin* and *decay*
> > (*Richard II*, iii, 2, 102)

> Death, desolation, *ruin* and *decay*
> > (*Richard III*, iv, 4, 409)

> Is yond despised and *ruin*ous man my lord?
> Full of *decay* and failing?
> > (*Timon of Athens*, iv, 3, 466)

[Note concomitant alliteration of *d* and *f*.]

2. beginn*ing* . . . end*ing* (opposite concepts, assonance)

> by this hot *beginning* we shall scarce bring it to a calm *ending*
> > (*The Famous Victories*, Scene 18, lines 31–32)

> The latter *end* of his commonwealth forgets the *beginning*.
> > (*Tempest*, ii, 1, 158)

> To show our simple skill,
> That is the true *beginning* of our *end*.
> > (*Midsummer Night's Dream*, v, 1, 110–11)

> I will tell *you the beginning*, and if it please your ladyships,
> *you* may *see the end*
> > (*As You Like It*, i, 2, 119)

To the latter *end* of a fray and the *beginning* of a feast
                              (*1 Henry IV*, IV, 2, 85)

We see yon*der the beginning of* the day, but I think *we* shall nev*er see the end of* it.
                              (*Henry V*, IV, 1, 91)

The other course
Will prove too bloody, and the *end* of it
Unknown to the *beginning*.
                              (*Coriolanus*, III, 1, 327–29)

3. protector . . . realm (related concepts)

for revengement I have chosen you to be my *Protector* over my *realm*
                    (*The Famous Victories*, Scene 9, lines 167–68)

thou art *Protector*,
And lookest to command the *Prince and realm*
                              (*1 Henry VI*, I, 1, 37)

There's none *protector* of the *realm* but I.
                              (*1 Henry VI*, I, 3, 12)

thou most usurping *pro*ditor,
And not *protector*, of the King or *realm*
                              (*1 Henry VI*, I, 3, 31–32)

he is *Protector* of the *realm*
                              (*1 Henry VI*, I, 3, 66)

Madam, I am *Protector* of the *realm*
                              (*2 Henry VI*, I, 3, 123)

The Duke is made *Protector* of the *realm*
                              (*3 Henry VI*, I, 1, 240)

4. *you . . . your kin* (related concepts, repetition)

I'll hang *you* and all *your kin*!
                    (*The Famous Victories*, Scene 1, lines 74–75)

in *you* to *your kin*
>   (*Richard III*, III, 7, 212)

5. *king . . . kingly* (related concepts, repetition)

> 'tis a *kingly resolution* and the *resolution* of a *king*
>   (*The Famous Victories*, Scene 14, lines 51–52)

> A *king, woe*'s *s*lave, shall *kingly woe* obey.
>   (*Richard II*, III, 2, 210)

> I give *th*ee *kingly th*anks,
> Because *th*is is in traffic of a *King*
>   (*1 Henry VI*, V, 3, 163)

> *More* like a *King, more kingly* in my thoughts
>   (*2 Henry VI*, V, 1, 29)

> The wrinkles in my *b*rows, n*ow* filled with *b*lood,
> Were *l*ikened oft to *kingly* sepulchres.
> For who *l*ived *king*, but *I* could dig his grave?
>   (*3 Henry VI*, V, 2, 19–21)

> Then I salute you with this *kingly* title—
> *L*ong *l*ive Richard, Eng*l*and's roya*l King*!
>   (*Richard III*, III, 7, 239–40)

6. *dead . . . d*rowsy (related concepts, alliteration)

> *d*rawing near of *drowsy* summer of *death*
>   (*The Famous Victories*, Scene 8, line 76)

> By the *dead* and *drowsy* fire
>   (*Midsummer Night's Dream*, V, 1, 399)

> The *o*rgans, though *d*efunct and *dead* bef*o*re,
> Br*ea*k up their *drowsy* grave and ne*w*ly m*o*ve
>   (*Henry V*, IV, 1, 21–22)

7. *a*horseback . . . *a*foot (opposite concepts, alliteration)

> we are *ahorseback* and they be *afoot*
>> (*The Famous Victories*, Scene 1, line 29)

> *O' horseback*, ye cuckoo, but *afoot* he will not budge *a foot*.
>> (*1 Henry IV*, 11, 4, 387)

8. *all* . . . wh*ole* (similar concepts, consonance)

> [See Item X, above.]

9. *trea*chery . . . *trea*son (related concepts, alliteration, consonance)

> view the place for fear of *treachery* and *treason*
>> (*The Famous Victories*, Scene 15, lines 47–48)

> By *treason*, falsehood and by *treachery*
>> (*1 Henry VI*, v, 4, 109)

10. *lay* . . . *lie* (alliteration, consonance)

> you must *lay* down *your sword*, or else they will not *lie* on *your sword*
>> (*The Famous Victories*, Scene 17, lines 12–13)

> It never yet did *h*urt
> To *lay* down *likeli*hoods and forms of *h*ope.
>> (*2 Henry IV*, 1, 3, 34–35)

> And wish h*er lays were* tuned *li*ke the *l*ark
>> (*Passionate Pilgrim*, 198)

> *T*heir smoo*th*ness, *li*ke a good*ly* champ*ai*gn pl*ai*n,
> *Lays* open all *th*e *little* worms
>> (*Lucrece*, 1247–48)

> [The curious phrase *all the* . . . *worms* approximates *all the* . . . *world;* see Item IX, above.]

Class Three

Paired words found in the canonical plays, The Famous Victories, *and elsewhere.*

1. *right* . . . *wrong* (opposite concepts, consonance)

    [See Item VIII, above.]

2. *jest* . . . *earnest* (opposite concepts, assonance)

    is it your man's quality to rob folks *in jest?*
    In faith, *h*e shall be *h*anged *in earnest.*
                            (*The Famous Victories*, Scene 4, lines 60–61)

    after *they* close*d in earnest, they* parte*d very fairly in jest*
                            (*Two Gentlemen of Verona*, II, 5, 13)

    Now your *jest* is *earnest.*
                            (*Comedy of Errors*, II, 2, 24)

    And given *in earnest* what I begged *in jest*
                            (*Richard III*, v, 1, 22)

    But, *t*urning these *jests* out of service, let us *t*alk in good
    earnest.
                            (*As You Like It*, I, 3, 25–26)

3. *weep* (tears) . . . *fountain* (related concepts)

    I will *weep d*ay and *n*ight un*til* the *fountain* be *d*ry *w*ith
    weeping
                            (*The Famous Victories*, Scene 8, lines 22–23)

    And in the *f*ountain shall we gaze so long
    *T*ill *t*he *f*resh *t*aste be *t*aken from *t*hat clearness,
    And made a *b*rine pit with our *b*itter *tears?*
                            (*Titus Andronicus*, III, 1, 127–29)

> *I will weep for nothing, like Diana in the fountain*
> > (*As You Like It*, IV, I, 153–54)

> Each cheek a *river running from a fount*
> With brinish current *downward flowed* apace
> > (*A Lover's Complaint*, 283–84)

4. bird . . . cage (related concepts)

> much like to a *bird* which hath escaped out of the *cage*
> > (*The Famous Victories*, Scene 9, lines 1–2)

> the field is honorable./And there was he [Jack Cade] born, under a hedge [like a *bird*], for his father had never a house but the *cage*.
> > (*2 Henry VI*, IV, 2, 52–56)

> He taught me how to know a man in love, in which *cage* of rushes I am sure you are not prisoner [like a *bird*].
> > (*As You Like It*, III, 2, 390)

> I am trusted with a muzzle, and enfranchised with a clog; therefore I have decreed not to sing [like a *bird*] in my *cage*.
> > (*Much Ado*, I, 3, 33–35)

> We two alone will sing like *birds* i' the *cage*.
> > (*King Lear*, V, 3, 9)

> Our *cage*/We make a choir as doth the prisoned *bird*
> > (*Cymbeline*, III, 3, 42)

5. devil . . . mischief (related concepts)

> the *devil*, which is master of all *mischief*
> > (*The Famous Victories*, Scene 6, line 30)

> Some airy *devil* hovers in the sky/And pours down *mischief*.
> > (*King John*, III, 2, 2–3)

> *that devil monk*,/Hopkins, *that made this mischief*
> > (*Henry VIII*, II, 1, 21–22)

6. rock . . . sleep (related concepts)

>   cause some music to *rock* me a-*sleep*
>   (*The Famous Victories*, Scene 8, lines 11, 78–79)

>   death *rock* me a*sleep*
>   (*2 Henry IV*, II, 4, 211)

>   [*Sleep*] *rock* his brains
>   In *c*radle of the *r*ude im*p*erious *s*urge
>   (*2 Henry IV*, III, 1, 19–20)

>   *rock* the ground whereon these *sleep*ers be
>   (*Midsummer Night's Dream*, IV, 1, 90)

7. *balls* (*walls*) . . . *brass* (consonance, with or without alliteration)

>   he *w*ill toss you *balls* of *brass*
>   (*The Famous Victories*, Scene 11, line 32)

>   As if this flesh which *walls* about our life
>   *W*ere *brass*
>   (*Richard II*, III, 2, 167–68)

>   *W*alls of *b*eaten *brass*
>   (*Julius Caesar*, I, 3, 93)

8. *down* and *die* (alliteration, consonance)

>   I will lay me *down* and *die*
>   (*The Famous Victories*, Scene 6, line 36)

>   sit him *down* and *die*
>   (*2 Henry IV*, III, 1, 56)

>   shall thereon fall *and die*
>   (*Lucrece*, 1139)

9. cr*ave* . . . h*ave* (related concepts, consonance)

> Ay, but *I love her*, and must *crave her*—
> Nay, *I love her*, and will *have her*!
> > (*The Famous Victories*, Scene 18, lines 47–48)

> He, none but *he*, shall *have her*,
> *Though* twenty *th*ousand *w*orthier *c*ome to *crave her*.
> > (*Merry Wives of Windsor*, IV, 4, 89–90)

> But I'll unto his *M*ajesty, and *crave*
> I *may have* liberty to venge this wrong.
> > (*1 Henry VI*, III, 4, 41)

10. seat [throne] . . . god (related concepts)

> Methought *his seat was like* the figure of *h*eaven, and *his*
> person *was like unto* a god.
> > (*The Famous Victories*, Scene 9, lines 24–25)

> I *s*aw young *H*arry . . .
> Rise from the ground *like* feathered Mercury [i.e., a *god*]
> And vaulted with *s*uch *ease into his seat*
> > (*1 Henry IV*, IV, 1, 104–7)

> With due ob*s*ervance of thy *godlike seat,*
> great Agamemnon .
> > (*Troilus and Cressida*, I, 3, 31)

> [Note concomitant *like* in these instances.]

11. *p*erverse . . . *p*eremptory (alliteration, assonance)

> *You* are very *peremptory* . . . /And *you* as *perverse*
> > (*The Famous Victories*, Scene 18, lines 23–25)

> If *I* were covetous, ambitious, or *perverse*
> As *he* will *have* me, *h*ow am *I* so *poor*?
> > (*1 Henry VI*, III, 1, 29–30)

And *perish ye*, with your audacious *prate*!
Presumptuous vassals, . . .
And *you*, my lords, methinks *you* do not well
To bear with their *perverse* objections, . . .
Let me *persuade* you take a better course.

(*1 Henry VI*, IV, 1, 124–32)

At lovers' *perjuries*
They say Jove laughs. O gentle Romeo,
If thou dost love, *pronounce* it faithfully.
Or *if thou think'st* I am too quickly won,
I'll frown and be *perverse*

(*Romeo and Juliet*, II, 2, 92–96)

Perverse it shall be where it shows most toward,
Put fear to valour

(*Venus and Adonis*, 1157–58)

Pernicious Protector, dangerous *peer*, . . .
What, Cardinal, is your *priesthood* grown *peremptory*?

(*2 Henry VI*, II, 1, 21–23)

How *proud*, how *peremptory*

(*2 Henry VI*, III, 1, 8)

I am *peremptory*.
My lord, I cannot be so soon *provided*.
Please you

(*Two Gentlemen of Verona*, I, 3, 71–73)

his discourse *peremptory*. . . . He is too
picked, too *spruce* . . . too *peregrinate*.

(*Love's Labor's Lost*, V, 1, 11)

I am as *peremptory* as she *proud*-minded

(*The Taming of the Shrew*, II, 1, 132)

your *presence* is too bold and *peremptory*

(*1 Henry IV*, I, 3, 17)

> Well, then, the *peace* . . .
> Pleaseth your Grace
> To a*ppoint* some of your Council *presently* . . .
> Pass our accept and *peremptory* answer.
>> (*Henry V*, v, 2, 75–82)

12. *represen*t . . . *person* (consonance, metathesis)

[See Item V, above.]

XVI. Fixed phrases of two or more words have, no doubt, always characterized both the common and the individual idiom of English-speaking peoples. Some of those that appear in *The Famous Victories* I take to be specifically Shakespearean. Others, even if they have some currency, have significance for this argument inasmuch as they are specifically characteristic both of the anonymous author and of Shakespeare.

Class One

Fixed phrases that may be specifically Shakespearean.

1. We few

> though *we* be *few*
>> (*The Famous Victories*, Scene 14, line 11)

> *We few*, *we* happy *few*
>> (*Henry V*, iv, 3, 60)

2. chafing with

> I had almost forgot the chiefest thing of all *with chafing with* this French ambassador
>> (*The Famous Victories*, Scene 9, lines 155–56)

The *troubled Tiber chafing with her* shores
                              (*Julius Caesar*, I, 2, 101)

3. take/took a box on the ear

what *a box on the ear* I *took* my Lord Chief Justice
                    (*The Famous Victories*, Scene 5, lines 2–3)

If he *took* you *a box o' th' ear*
                              (*Measure for Measure*, II, 1, 189)

I will *take* thee *a box on the ear*
                              (*Henry V*, IV, 1, 231)

I have sworn to *take* him *a box o' th' ear*
                              (*Henry V*, IV, 7, 133)

4. stand/stay prating here

we stand prating here too long
                    (*The Famous Victories*, Scene 5, lines 57–58)

Why *stay we prating here*?
                              (*Coriolanus*, I, 1, 49)

5. stand upon thorns

I *stand upon thorns* till the crown be on my head
                    (*The Famous Victories*, Scene 5, lines 50–51)

The roses fearfully *on thorns* did *stand*
                              (*Sonnet XCIX*, 8)

But Oh, the *thorns* we *stand upon*!
                              (*Winter's Tale*, IV, 4, 596)

6. man/fellow of his/my hands

I tell you, *he* is a *man of his hands*.
                    (*The Famous Victories*, Scene 4, lines 47–48)

The worst that they can say of me is that I am a second brother
and that I am a proper *fellow of my hands*

(*2 Henry IV*, II, 2, 70–72)

7. too precise/too precisely

too precise in this matter

(*The Famous Victories*, Scene 3, line 54)

thinking *too precisely* on the event

(*Hamlet*, IV, 4, 41)

8. this month

I shall feel it *this month*

(*The Famous Victories*, Scene 1, line 34)

whereon *this month* I have been hammering

(*Two Gentlemen of Verona*, I, 3, 18)

where hast thou been *this month*?

(*1 Henry IV*, II, 4, 474–75)

9. high-minded

a *h*aughty and *high-minded* prince

(*The Famous Victories*, Scene 11, lines 33–34)

this *high-minded* strumpet

(*1 Henry VI*, I, 5, 12)

10. bloody soldier

I was called "the *bloody soldier*"

(*The Famous Victories*, Scene 19, lines 13–14)

The *bl*ind and *bloody soldier* with foul hand

(*Henry V*, III, 3, 34)

> *W*hat *bloody* man is t*h*at? . . . *Th*is is the sergeant
> *W*ho like a good and hardy *soldier* fought
>
> (*Macbeth*, I, 2, 1–4)

11. bloody fray

> such a *bloody fray* as passeth
>
> (*The Famous Victories*, Scene 2, line 106)

> *Death* ha*th* not *s*truck *s*o fat a *deer* today,
> *Th*ough many *dearer*, in t*h*is *bloody fray.*
>
> (*1 Henry IV*, v, 4, 107–8)

> After the *bloody fray* at Wakefield fought
>
> (*3 Henry VI*, II, 1, 107)

> who *b*egan this *bloody fray*
>
> (*Romeo and Juliet*, III, 1, 156)

12. liege people

> I am one of the King's *liege people*
>
> (*The Famous Victories*, Scene 2, line 79)

> Which if he take, shall quite un*people* her
> Of *liegers*
>
> (*Cymbeline*, I, 5, 79–80)

13. villainous trick

> a *villainous* part of me . . . a *trick* of youth
>
> (*The Famous Victories*, Scene 1, lines 9–11)

> a *villainous trick* of thine eye
>
> (*1 Henry IV*, II, 4, 445)

14. penny ransom

> pay one *penny ransom* for my body
>
> (*The Famous Victories*, Scene 14, lines 48–49)

ask me for one *penny* cost
To *ransom* home revolted *Mortimer*.

                    (*1 Henry IV*, 1, 3, 91–92)

Class Two

Fixed phrases found in The Famous Victories, *in Shake-speare, and elsewhere.*

1. old acquaintance

I can get anything of them for *old acquaintance*
                    (*The Famous Victories*, Scene 9, lines 5–6)

What, *old acquaintance*! Could not all this flesh
Keep in a *li*ttle *li*fe?

                    (*1 Henry IV*, v, 4, 102)

to see how many of my *old acquaintance* are dead
                    (*2 Henry IV*, III, 2, 37–38)

let our *old acquaintance* be renewed
                    (*2 Henry IV*, III, 2, 314)

How does my *old acquaintance* of this isle?
                    (*Othello*, II, 1, 205)

I urged our *old acquaintance*
                    (*Coriolanus*, v, 1, 10)

2. poor men

you seem to be *poor men*
                    (*The Famous Victories*, Scene 2, lines 54–55)

He may mean more than we *poor men* do know.
                    (*1 Henry VI*, 1, 2, 122)

Thou hast appointed justices of peace to call *poor men* before
them
>   (*2 Henry VI*, IV, 7, 46)

Long sitting to determine *poor men*'s causes
Hath made me full of sickness
>   (*2 Henry VI*, IV, 7, 93)

a many *poor men*'s lives saved
>   (*Henry V*, IV, 1, 127–28)

though I be but a *poor man*
>   (*Much Ado*, III, 5, 29–30)

3. *say true*

Faith, Ned, thou *sayest true*.
>   (*The Famous Victories*, Scene 1, line 12)

By the Lord, thou *sayest true*, lad.
>   (*1 Henry IV*, I, 2, 45)

[Cf. *ibid.*, II, 4, 400; III, 3, 149]

I say mine eye *saith true*
>   (*Sonnet CXIV*, 3)

4. crave pardon

And could not I *crave pardon* for all?
>   (*The Famous Victories*, Scene 8, line 18)

I then *crave pardon* of your majesty
>   (*3 Henry VI*, IV, 6, 8)

I *crave* your *pardon*.
>   (*Comedy of Errors*, I, 2, 26)

I *crave* your Honor's *pardon*.
>   (*Measure for Measure*, II, 2, 14)

I *crave* their *pardons.*
> (*Coriolanus,* III, 1, 65)

I *crave* your Highness' *pardon.*
> (*Antony and Cleopatra,* II, 5, 98)

5. let me alone with him/them

if the villains come, *let me alone with them!*
> (*The Famous Victories,* Scene 1, line 31)

Let me alone with him.
> (*King John,* IV, 1, 85)

6. give occasion

a rude youth, and likely to *give occasion*
> (*The Famous Victories,* Scene 3, lines 9–10)

fee'd every slight *occasion* that could but niggardly *give* me
sight of her
> (*Merry Wives of Windsor,* II, 2, 204)

And nature, stronger than his just *occasion,*
Made him *give* battle
> (*As You Like It,* IV, 3, 130–31)

And when I *give occasion* of offence,
Then let me die
> (*3 Henry VI,* I, 3, 44)

the least *occasion* that may *give* me
Remembrance
> (*Henry VIII,* III, 2, 7)

a very little thief of *occasion* will rob you of a great deal of
patience. *Give* your dispositions the reins
> (*Coriolanus,* II, 1, 31–33)

an you will *give* me *occasion*
> (*Romeo and Juliet,* III, 1, 44–45)

Could you not take some *occasion* without *giving*?
> (*Romeo and Juliet*, III, 1, 46–47)

7. it skills not

Well, *it skills not*; I'll save the base villain's life, if I may.
> (*The Famous Victories*, Scene 1, line 26)

It skills not greatly who impugns our doom
> (*2 Henry VI*, III, 1, 281)

it skills not much when they are delivered
> (*Twelfth Night*, V, 1, 295)

whate'er he be,
It skills not much, we'll fit him to our turn
> (*Taming of the Shrew*, III, 2, 133–34)

8. it boots not

it boots me *not* to take any physic
> (*The Famous Victories*, Scene 8, lines 1–2)

It boots thee *not* to be compassionate.
> (*Richard II*, I, 3, 174)

it boots thee *not*, proud Queen
> (*3 Henry VI*, I, 4, 125)

9. this gear

and all *this gear*
> (*The Famous Victories*, Scene 5, line 56)

[Bartlett cites 8 instances of the idiom in Shakespeare.]

10. in/on any ground

I dare encounter him *in any ground* of the world
> (*The Famous Victories*, Scene 11, lines 56–57)

on any plot of *ground* in Christendom
> (*1 Henry VI*, ɪɪ, 4, 89)

on any ground that I am ruler of
> (*2 Henry VI*, ɪɪɪ, 2, 296)

No man so potent breathes up*on* the *ground*
> (*1 Henry IV*, ɪv, 1, 11)

any vantage of *ground*
> (*2 Henry IV*, ɪɪ, 1, 85)

an inch of *any ground*
> (*2 Henry IV*, ɪv, 1, 109)

11. we wait upon your Grace

We are ready to *wait upon your Grace.*
> (*The Famous Victories*, Scene 1, line 87)

We wait upon your Grace.
> (*Richard III*, ɪɪ, 1, 140)

12. fresh supply

a *fresh supply* with his daughter
> (*The Famous Victories*, Scene 18, lines 42–43)

this noble Queen
And Prince shall follow with a *fresh supply*
> (*3 Henry VI*, ɪɪɪ, 3, 236–37)

13. to ward

we sent him *to ward*
> (*The Famous Victories*, Scene 3, line 38)

ere they will have me go *to ward*,
They'll pawn their swords
> (*2 Henry VI*, v, 1, 112)

14. thrice-

> *thrice*-unhappy
> > (*The Famous Victories*, Scene 8, line 12)

[Bartlett cites 19 different adjectival compounds of this type in Shakespeare: *thrice*-blessed, *thrice*-crowned, *thrice*-double, etc.]

15. part about

> I delight as much in their tongues as any *part about* them
> > (*The Famous Victories*, Scene 1, lines 85–86)

> every *part about* you blasted with antiquity
> > (*2 Henry IV*, I, 2, 207)

16. (n)arrant whore

> She's a *narrant whore*
> > (*The Famous Victories*, Scene 7, line 6)

> Fortune, that *arrant whore*
> > (*King Lear*, II, 4, 52)

17. at host

> are you *at host* with me?
> > (*The Famous Victories*, Scene 18, line 86)

> Your goods that lay *at host*, sir, in the Centaur.
> > (*Comedy of Errors*, V, 1, 410)

18. conscience accuseth

> My *conscience accuseth* me.
> > (*The Famous Victories*, Scene 6, line 13)

> A man cannot steal but it [*conscience*] *accuseth* him
> > (*Richard III*, I, 4, 138–39)

*   *   *

In retrospect, the evidence presented in this chapter will no doubt seem somewhat heterogeneous. Every item, however, has appeared to me in some way significant as substantiation of this argument. I do not suppose the various items to have equal weight. Persons better read in Elizabethan literature than I may be able to show that some of the alleged Shakespeareanisms are not in fact such. I do not expect my case to suffer much from such discoveries.

I have sought to show that since the language of the canonical plays very often resembles that of *The Famous Victories*, we may reasonably suppose that Shakespeare wrote the old play. Sometimes I have argued the other way around, but I have in general avoided that procedure. I must admit to having little patience with those who think that because Shakespeare's language on occasion resembles that of other writers, we must entertain the possibility that the canonical plays were, as a whole or in part, written by one or more of these. Shakespeare was, of course, an accomplished mimic.[16] Actually, his more creative imitation is of himself.

---

[16] When he imitates another writer, he tends simply to borrow words and phrases; one seldom observes imitation of the aural phenomena which I have repeatedly noted in the relationships we have studied. This point could be exemplified by consideration of the "parallelisms" noted by Hoffman, pp. 203 ff., between Shakespeare and Marlowe.

FACTS AND INFERENCES

Veritas virescit vulnere
(the motto of Thomas Creed)

That Shakespeare wrote *The Famous Victories* cannot be established by documentation. Nevertheless, for the sake of completeness, an investigation of the data amenable to the customary tests of historical criticism must now be undertaken. I may fairly claim in advance that I have discovered nothing to disprove my view. I hope to show, indeed, that the evidence strengthens the likelihood that Shakespeare wrote the old play.

Study of *The Famous Victories* has been stymied for nearly four decades—in fact, since two distinguished scholars, Alfred Pollard and John Dover Wilson, set forth their opinion that the play cannot be thought of as the immediate source of Shakespeare's *1* and *2 Henry IV* and *Henry V*. They asserted that all four must derive from an ultimate lost original, a play in two parts, of which *The Famous Victories* is "clearly" an abridgement.[1] This conclusion

---

[1] Pollard and Wilson, pp. 18, 134.

was by no means inevitable. It is true that a now lost version of *1* and *2 Henry IV*, with Sir John Oldcastle's name in place of Falstaff's, existed as early as 1592;[2] but *The Famous Victories*, as will be shown, dates from 1586;[3]—it is more likely that the version of 1592 and the extant trilogy were all in some degree derivative from it. The effect of the conjectures of Pollard and Wilson was to suggest the inferiority of the received text of *The Famous Victories*. Thus, in 1924, A. E. Morgan undertook to show that it is badly botched; he imagined it "a roughly shortened form of a verse play."[4] To establish the corruption of the text, he announced various difficulties of interpretation in the first half of the piece.[5] It is a comment on the ready acquiescence of scholarship when no considerable matters appear to be at stake, that thirty years passed before his findings were

---

[2] Over twenty verbal parallels, which can only be understood as echoes of a text (or texts) similar to those we know, have been found in the writings of Thomas Nash from 1592 to 1594. These have been collected by Wilson; cf. New Cambridge ed. *1 Henry IV*, pp. 191 ff. In 1592 George Harvey ridicules the bombast of Nash (and Shakespeare) thus: "Never child so delighted in his rattling bauble; as some old Lads of the Castle have sported themselves with their rapping babble" (Harvey, p. 74). This echoes Prince Hal's "my old lad of the castle," a phrase vestigially surviving in *1 Henry IV*, I, 2, 47, in allusion to Oldcastle, predecessor of Falstaff. (See below, pp. 177–79.) Harvey can only have taken it from Shakespeare, for it is meaningless except as an allusion. The fact that a version of *Henry IV* was in existence thus early is further certified by mention of "hypocritical hotspurs" in Nash, I, 161, and (echoing him) in Harvey, p. 54. A blank verse fragment of twelve lines, which may well belong to the lost version, is preserved in the hand of the dramatist John Day; cf. Hemingway, p. 392.

[3] See below, pp. 180–82.

[4] Morgan, p. 8.

[5] Morgan, p. 9, explains that he is not concerned with the relation of *The Famous Victories* to *Henry V*.

challenged. C. A. Greer has now indicated something of his carelessness—and even perversity—in reading.[6] There is no substantiation whatever for Morgan's allegation that there are 250 lines of hidden poetry in the play's manifest prose.[7]

Over the years, nevertheless, Morgan's opinion that *The Famous Victories* is a bungled version of an earlier original has been accepted.[8] Wilson, ratifying Morgan, has elaborated his position with the statement that the play is a "bad" quarto: "It is a memorial reconstruction, by a touring troupe attached, as the title page shows, to the Queen's men, of a full length play or plays." [9]

Against such confident affirmation it may be folly, if not presumption, to protest. I should like to urge, however, that:

1) There is nothing to indicate that the play is an abstract of two or more plays. (Nothing need be inferred from the mere brevity of the text, or from the fact that it deals with Henry of Monmouth both as prince and as king.)

---

[6] Greer (February, 1954), p. 53: "Most of Morgan's evidence simply does not exist, is far-fetched or strained after, or will not hold up." Greer is, however, troubled about the double role of Tarlton in the performance at the Bull; see below, n. 51.

[7] Morgan's contention that there are numerous verse "fossils" in the prose of *1 Henry IV* was rejected by E. K. Chambers (1930), I 233–34, 383, on the argument that the criteria were unreliable. Cf. also Greer, *op. cit.*, p. 54. In the opinion of Hopkinson, p. iv, the use of prose in *The Famous Victories* is "a singular and important fact in determining the date of writing, for it shows conclusively that it must have been composed . . . between 1585 and 1588, with the probability that the earlier date is nearer the mark."

[8] Cf. Chambers (1930), I, 393; Craig, pp. 44, 675.

[9] Wilson (1945), p. 10. However, Tillyard, p. 149, describes *The Famous Victories* as "a kind of dramatic Lamb's Tale—of Shakespeare's early plays on the reigns of Henry IV and Henry V."

2) There is nothing to indicate that the received text was put together by a touring troupe. (We know, to be sure, that in 1594 the Queen's men "broke and went into the country," [10] but Creed presumably bought the play from them prior to that, since he registered it for publication on May 14.)

3) There is nothing to indicate that the play is a memorial reconstruction.

4) It is incorrect to describe the text as corrupt. [11] (The quarto of 1598 occasionally shows wrongly assigned speeches, inaccurate stage directions, misspellings, and the like. These are printer's errors which the quarto of 1617 in several instances corrects.)

1. THE TITLE PAGES

The title pages of the two extant early editions of *The Famous Victories* offer us the following information: the text was printed in 1598 by Thomas Creed, "as it was played by the Queen's Majesty's Players," and, in 1617, by Bernard Alsop, "as it was acted by the King's Majesty's Servants." The authorship of the play was in neither instance specified. That need cause us no surprise, for it was not yet routine to indicate authorship on title pages.

In this argument, the year 1598 has interest and significance, for, by conservative opinion, it marks the full establishment of Shakespeare's reputation. In that year four of

---

[10] Henslowe, I, 27.

[11] Greer, *op. cit.*, p. 54, offers substantiation on this point: "The text of the *Victories*, I find, reads rather smoothly and uninterruptedly. . . . For the time of its composition and use on the stage it is not crude at all."

FAMOVS VIC-
tories of Henry the
fifth:

Containing the Honou-
rable Battell of Agin-court:

As it was plaide by the Queenes Maiesties
Players.

LONDON
Printed by Thomas Creede, **1598.**

The Title Page of *The Famous Victories* (edition of 1598)

Reproduced by permission of the Bodleian Library, Oxford.

the canonical plays were issued in quarto texts: *Richard II* (in two printings), *Richard III* (printed by Creed), *Love's Labor's Lost*, and *1 Henry IV*. The first octavo of *The Rape of Lucrece* also appeared, and *The Merchant of Venice* was entered in the Stationers' Register for publication. At the same time the proliferation of references to Shakespeare in contemporary documents began, including Francis Meres' celebrated—and incomplete—listing of the comedies and tragedies to date.[12]

It is true that in printing (for Andrew Wise) what was the second quarto of *Richard III*, Creed indicated that play as being "By William Shake-speare." [13] With William White, the printer of the first extant edition of *Love's Labor's Lost*, he thus shares the initiative in rightly ascribing one of the dramatist's plays on its title page. But Wise, at about the same time, was publishing the first quarto of *The History of Henry the Fourth;*[14] perhaps he persuaded Creed that it was to their common advantage not to specify the authorship of either play. Both pieces would in any case be well known as Shakespeare's. The older, "containing the honorable battle of Agincourt," had been on the boards for more than a decade, but was certainly inferior. The more recent, "with the battle at Shrewsbury, between the King and Lord Henry Percy, surnamed Henry Hotspur of the North" and also "with the humorous conceits of Sir John Falstaff," lacked, Wise may yet have regretted, the notorious

---

[12] Meres includes "Henry the 4" among the tragedies. He omits the three parts of *Henry VI* and *The Taming of the Shrew*. Cf. Chambers (1930), II, 194.

[13] It may have been his intention simply to distinguish it from the *True Tragedy of Richard III*, which he had himself registered and printed in 1594. See below, p. 169.

[14] The play was registered on February 25, 1598.

and now suppressed Sir John Oldcastle—who, in fact, catches a prospective reader's eye on the first page of *The Famous Victories*.[15] Each publication perhaps stood to lose something if its rival alone claimed Shakespeare's authorship, and the idea of attributing both plays to his hand evidently did not commend itself.[16]

Among Elizabethan stationers Thomas Creed was particularly enterprising and, it seems, somewhat unscrupulous.[17] Already in 1594, according to Chambers' reckoning, he had acquired for publication as many as ten plays; four of these at least, including *The Famous Victories*, came from the stock of the moribund Queen's Players.[18] From this time Creed showed a particular interest in Shakespeare, and for years, the facts suggest, he pursued a clever course in capitalizing on the dramatist's successes.

Thus, when Creed's career as printer of plays began, also in 1594, he issued for Thomas Millington,[19] without indication of authorship, *The First Part of the Contention betwixt the Two Houses of York and Lancaster*, now usually described as a reconstruction of *2 Henry VI*, which by this time must have been familiar.[20] During the same year, and presumably after the first production of *Richard III*,[21] Creed registered and printed the anonymous *True Tragedy of Richard III*, an old Queen's play of which Shakespeare

---

[15] It may be doubted that Oldcastle had a part in the 1586 text. See below, pp. 177-78.

[16] Hopkinson, p. ii, believes Creed printed *The Famous Victories* to take advantage of the popularity of *1 Henry IV*.

[17] Maxwell, p. 19.

[18] Chambers (1923), III, 184.

[19] Millington's interest in Shakespeare resembled Creed's, but he was less active; cf. Halliday, p. 414.

[20] Chambers (1930), I, 281 ff.

[21] Chambers (1930), I, 303.

had made considerable use.[22] It seems likely that in both of these undertakings the publishers counted on deceiving buyers, in the belief that they might acquire texts of plays recently seen in the theaters. Creed probably had similar motives when, on May 14, 1594, he registered *The Famous Victories of Henry the Fifth*.[23] As we have indicated, a predecessor of *1* and *2 Henry IV* was abroad by 1592.

In 1595 Creed continued this same pattern of activity. After *The Comedy of Errors* had been staged,[24] he licensed and printed William Warner's English version of Plautus' *Menaechmi*, on the Latin original of which Shakespeare's farce had largely been based. He also licensed and printed *Locrine*, describing it as "Newly set forth, overseen, and corrected, by W. S." Whether he meant to attribute the play or the corrections—or both—to Shakespeare is uncertain; no one would make either claim today.[25]

In 1598, then, Creed printed *The Famous Victories* and the second quarto of *Richard III*, which was ascribed to Shakespeare. Three more quartos of *Richard III* were to come from Creed's press, in 1602, 1605, and 1612, each properly ascribed. The rest of the printer's record, as it relates to the dramatist, shows that he was quite inconsistent in the matter of ascription. In 1599 he printed for Cuthbert Burby the second quarto of *Romeo and Juliet*, declaring the play to be "Newly corrected, augmented, and amended," but failing to cite Shakespeare as author or reviser. Furthermore, following the staging of *Henry V* in 1599, he produced two inferior quartos without attribution: one, in 1600,

---

[22] Churchill, pp. 497–524.

[23] Daniel, p. iii, thinks the play may first have been printed in 1594.

[24] *The Comedy of Errors* was presented at Gray's Inn on December 28, 1594; cf. Chambers (1930), p. 310.

[25] Maxwell, pp. 64 ff.

for Millington and Busby; the other, in 1602, for Pavier. In 1602, on the other hand, he ascribed to Shakespeare a wretched text of *The Merry Wives of Windsor*. Finally, in 1605, without excuse known to posterity, Creed indicated *The London Prodigal* as Shakespeare's.[26]

In 1616, the year of Shakespeare's death, Creed is known to have taken Bernard Alsop as his partner, and in the following year Alsop reprinted *The Famous Victories*. Alsop did not claim the play for Shakespeare, perhaps because by now four editions of *1 Henry IV* had been unequivocally identified. Yet Alsop may well have hoped to profit by a traditional association.

By present-day professional standards the record of Thomas Creed is quite obviously open to criticism. We owe him much, nevertheless. From 1594, as publisher and printer, he followed Shakespeare's career closely. Although Creed must have made a good thing of it, Shakespeare can have had no control over his procedures. He was perhaps often displeased with Creed, probably never consulted; he can scarcely have made any money directly from Creed's ventures. It is significant for our argument, I think, that it was this man, early confident of the salability of plays rightly or wrongly associated with Shakespeare, who registered, printed, and published *The Famous Victories*.[27]

---

[26] Cf. Maxwell, p. 13.

[27] The list of books published by Creed includes many celebrated titles: *The Shepherd's Calendar* (1586, 1597); *The Defense of Poesie* (1595); *Colin Clout's Come Home Again* (1595); *The Second Part of the Faerie Queene* (1596); *Mother Bombie* (1598); *A Looking Glass for London and England* (1598); *Green's Groatsworth of Wit* (1600), etc. Cf. Ames, II, 1279 ff.

THE
FAMOVS VIC-
TORIES OF HENRY
The fifth.

CONTAINING
the Honourable Battell of
AGIN-COVRT.

*As it was Acted by the Kinges Maiesties
Seruants.*

LONDON
Imprinted by *Barnard Alsop,* **dwelling**
in Garter place in Barbican.
1 6 1 7.

The Title Page of *The Famous Victories* (edition of 1617)
Reproduced by permission of The Folger Shakespeare Library.

The title pages tell us that this play had been acted by the Queen's Players, as of 1598, and by the King's Majesty's Servants, as of 1617. The latter was, of course, Shakespeare's company. It seems to me likely that acting rights had been retained by the play's author—or its author's company—through the years; and likely also, since it gave the gist of three popular plays, that it should have held a certain vogue throughout Shakespeare's life.[28]

That the play earlier belonged to the repertory of the Queen's, there can be no doubt. This celebrated company dated from 1583, when it had been selected, at Elizabeth's command, from the existing groups.[29] For many years it played every winter at Court and in the City, traveling during the summer.[30] It has often been maintained that Shakespeare could have been enlisted by the Queen's at the start of his career. The idea perhaps goes back to Nicholas Rowe's *Life* (1709):

He was received into the company then in being, at first in a very mean rank; but his admirable wit and the natural turn of it to the stage soon distinguished him, if not as an extraordinary actor, yet as an excellent writer.[31]

Malone proposes that Shakespeare may have joined the Queen's when they played at Stratford, perhaps as early as 1586.[32] If Rowe meant—and was indeed right—that Shake-

---

[28] Chambers (1923), II, 202, is skeptical of Alsop's motives in printing the play: "It was to pass as *Henry V;* obviously the King's men never acted it, *Henry V* being in existence." The verdict is perhaps too abrupt.

[29] Chambers (1923), II, 104 ff.

[30] In London the Queen's was licensed to play "at the signs of the Bull in Bishopsgate Street, and the sign of the Bell in Gracious Street and nowhere else within this City"; cf. Halliday, p. 521.

[31] Chambers (1930), II, 265.

[32] Malone, II, 166.

speare was first employed in this particular company, his affirmation that he "soon distinguished" himself as a playwright should also be considered seriously. It has too often been surmised that Shakespeare, being a rustic, can only have begun in the theater as an actor!

We know a good deal about the repertory of the Queen's. Fourteen of their plays have come down to us: four by Robert Green, one each by George Peele and Robert Wilson, and the rest anonymous. As in the case of *The Famous Victories*, several have obvious relevance to the study of Shakespeare: notably, *1* and *2 The Troublesome Reign of King John*, *The True Tragedy of Richard III*, and *King Leir*.

That Shakespeare was early acquainted with Richard Tarlton, the chief comedian of the Queen's ("for a wondrous plentiful pleasant extemporal wit, he was the wonder of his time" [33]), has been now and then suggested.[34] There exists in support of this proposal Hamlet's tribute to the otherwise unidentified Yorick: [35]

I knew him, Horatio—a fellow of infinite jest, of most excellent fancy. . . . Where be your gibes now? Your gambols? Your songs? Your flashes of merriment that were wont to set the table on a roar?

(*Hamlet* v, 1, 202 ff.)

The reader of *Tarlton's Jests* will be inclined to agree that this piece of reminiscence, a bit inorganic in the play, may be a tribute to Shakespeare's departed colleague.

It was perhaps customary at one time to associate Shake-

---

[33] Stow (1615), p. 697. For the life of Tarlton, see Lee, *DNB, s.v.*, "Richard Tarlton (d. 1588)."

[34] Cf. Monaghan, p. 359.

[35] The name of Yorick is, I believe, a conflation of York and Warwick; cf. Pitcher, p. 11.

Tarltons Iests.

Drawne into thefe three parts.

- **1 His Court-wittie Iefts**
- **2 His found Cittie Iefts.**
- **3 His Country prettie Iefts.**

Full of Delight, Wit, and honeft Myrth.

RICHARD TARLETON
one of the first Actors in
SHAKESPEARS PLAYS.

An eighteenth-century
engraving based on the
woodcut of 1613

LONDON,
Printed for *Iohn Budge,* and are to be fold at his fhop, at the
great South duore of Paules. **1613.**

The Title Page of *Tarleton's Jests* (edition of
1613), From the unique copy in The Folger
Shakespeare Library.

Both reproduced by permission of The Folger Shakespeare Library.

speare and Tarlton. Thomas Fuller, for example, does just that. Having reported an epitaph upon the celebrated zany (*Hic situs est cuius poterat vox, actio, vultus,/Ex Heraclito reddere Democritum*) and averred that "the self-same words, spoken by another, would hardly move a merry man to smile, which uttered by him would force a sad soul to laughter," he repeats himself in commenting upon "our Shakespeare":

Heraclitus himself (I mean if secret and unseen) might afford to smile at his comedies, they were so merry; and Democritus scarce forbear to sigh at his tragedies, they were so mournful.[36]

We may also adduce, for whatever it may be worth, the subscription found, with an eighteenth-century engraving based on an early woodcut, showing Tarlton with tabor and pipe: "RICHARD TARLTON one of the first Actors in SHAKESPEARS PLAYS." [37] We do not know who printed this, nor on whose authority the assertion was made. It means—if it is reliable—that plays of Shakespeare were being performed by the Queen's before September 3, 1588, the date of Tarlton's death. Competent authority does not place any of the canonical plays as early as that.

It happens that it is possible to assert with assurance that Tarlton performed in *The Famous Victories*. And the role of Derick (nickname for Richard) would seem to have been created precisely for him.

---

[36] Fuller, III, 139–40, 284–85.

[37] Prints of the engraving may be seen at the Folger and Huntington Libraries. I first noticed it in reproduction in Craig, p. 56. The original woodcut appears on the title page of the 1613 edition of *Tarlton's Jests;* see below, n. 50. Both have been reproduced here on page 175.

2. SIGNIFICANT DATES

I have said that the date of licensing *The Famous Victories* for publication is firmly fixed: May 14, 1594. Since earlier productions of the play are on record, there is no reason to debate whether a reference to a "new" play, called "Harry the v," cited in Henslowe's *Diary* as being acted by the Lord Admiral's men at the Rose on November 28, 1595, concerns *The Famous Victories*.[38] It is clear that ours is a much older play, from the repertory of the Queen's.

On the other hand, one topical reference in the text of 1598 cannot be earlier than October 22, 1596.[39] Further alterations may have occurred about that time. The Puritan William Brooke, Lord Cobham, occupied the office of Lord Chamberlain from August 8, 1596, to March 5, 1597. It may well have been during this time that Shakespeare was badgered into revising *Henry IV* by deleting Sir John Oldcastle;[40] the historical Oldcastle, an ancestor of the Cobhams, was remembered as a Protestant martyr.[41] It is likely

---

[38] Greg (Henslowe, II, 177–78) and Morgan, p. 12, believe that the Admiral's men appropriated the play and revised it; hence Henslowe's "new." Morgan thinks our version is the botched Admiral's play (falsely ascribed to the Queen's); Greg decides, however, that Creed must have printed the play "from the original MS."

[39] Reference to the "Earl of Nottingham" (Scene 14, line 16) can only be to the Elizabethan holder of that title (conferred on the date cited above). See below, pp. 189–90.

[40] Wilson (1945), pp. 13–14, presents evidence for the opinion that William Brooke was involved in this matter, rather than his son Henry, as has sometimes been supposed.

[41] The chronicler Edward Hall, an ardent Protestant, shows sympathy with Oldcastle, thus:

During this first year of the reign of Henry V, Sir John Oldcastle, which by his wife was called Lord Cobham, a valiant captain and

that Thomas Creed—or some hack writer in his employ—
undertook to make room for Oldcastle in *The Famous Victories* to enhance its attractiveness to the public. The original companions of Prince Henry had been designated, I
take it, as Ned, Tom, and perhaps Jockey (nickname for
John).[42] If he appeared in the original version, Jockey was,
I suggest, not identified with Sir John Oldcastle until the
edition of 1598; in support of this it may be remarked that
he suggests little of the character of the comical Oldcastle-
Falstaff as we know him in *1* and *2 Henry IV*.[43] All in
all, I incline to the view that there was neither John Oldcastle nor Jockey in the original version of *The Famous
Victories*.[44]

---

an hardy gentleman, was accused to the Archbishop of Canterbury
of certain points of heresy, which bishop, knowing him to be
highly in the King's favor, declared to his Highness the whole accusation (f. HV, ii, *verso*).

Perhaps the notion that Oldcastle enjoyed the King's friendship had
its origin here.

[42] See Explanatory Notes: Scene 1, *Ned* and *Tom;* also below,
n. 44.

[43] Monaghan, pp. 354–55, however, is of the opinion that "In the
old drama several speeches by Sir John Oldcastle [i.e., Jockey]—
showing the acknowledged coward and bombastic comedian—were
probably enough to suggest to the poet the creation of a comic companion for the prince."

[44] In each of the three appearances of Jockey-Oldcastle there are
makeshift awkwardnesses. In Scene 1, the identity of Sir John is
established in advance of his appearance; the stage direction calls,
however, for Jockey, and the Prince thereafter addresses him by that
name. In Scene 4, his omission is curious. In Scene 5, his unmotivated
separate arrival may be an afterthought; some of his speeches are
there attributed to him as John Oldcastle, some as Jockey. In Scene
10 (as we have it), although Jockey comes on with the other Knights,
the King speaks only to Ned and Tom in dismissing them from his
company.

Any critic unimpressed with the cogency of this last suggestion must, in justice, face a rather startling alternative. There exists a letter of Richard James, written to Sir Harry Bourchier after November 9, 1621, in which it is stated, "that in Shakespeare's first show of Harry the Fifth, the person with which he undertook to play a buffoon was not Falstaff, but Sir John Oldcastle." [45] When I first noticed this passage, it appeared to me conclusive proof that Shakespeare wrote *The Famous Victories*. The phrasing is, however, unsatisfactory. James may have been familiar only with the lost play of 1592.[46] But if so, is it conceivable that it was called *Henry V*? Can it have covered the entire span of events in *The Famous Victories*? On the other hand, if James knew the old play, how could he describe Oldcastle as its buffoon? Is it to be supposed that he confused Oldcastle with Derick? Amid these uncertainties I have felt justified in calling upon James for only moral support of my conviction of Shakespeare's authorship of the disputed play.

That *The Famous Victories* somewhat antedated Creed's registration of the play is the probable inference of the following passage from Thomas Nash's *Pierce Penniless* (1592):

. . . what a glorious thing it is to have Henry V represented on the stage, leading the French king prisoner, and forcing him and the Dolphin to swear fealty! "Aye but" (will they say) "what do we get by it?" Respecting neither the right of fame that is due to true nobil-

---

[45] Chambers (1930), II, 242. Sir Harry, it appears, was knighted on the date indicated above. James (1592–1638) was an antiquarian of considerable learning, librarian to Sir Robert Cotton. The commendatory verses, "On worthy Master Shakespeare and his poems," prefixed to the Folio of 1632 and signed "I.M.S." (JAMES?), have sometimes been ascribed to him.

[46] See above, n. 2.

ity deceased, nor what hopes of eternity are to be proposed to adven-
turous minds, to encourage them forward . . .[47]

It is true that in our play the French King does not in fact
swear fealty, as do the Dauphin and the Duke of Burgundy,
but this need mean no more than that Nash's memory was
rusty.[48]

A reference in *The Famous Victories* to "our old host's
at Faversham" (Scene 1, lines 79–80) may be topical, for the
Queen's played in that town in 1586, 1588, and 1591.[49] In
any case, we have certain knowledge that the play was produced in London some months before March 10, 1588:

At the Bull at Bishopsgate was a play of Henry the Fifth, wherein
the Judge was to take a box on the ear; and because he was absent
that should take the blow, Tarlton himself, ever forward to please,
took upon him to play the same Judge, besides his own part of the
Clown: and Knell, then playing Henry the Fifth, hit Tarlton a sound
box indeed, which made the people laugh the more because it was he,
but anon the Judge goes in, and immediately Tarlton in his clown's
clothes comes out, and asks the actors what news. "Ay," saith one,
"hadst thou been here thou shouldst have seen Prince Henry hit the
Judge a terrible box on the ear!" "What, man?" said Tarlton, "Strike
a Judge?" "It is truth, in faith," said the other. "No other like," said
Tarlton, "and it could not be but terrible to the Judge, when the report so terrifies me that methinks the blow remains still on my cheek,
that it burns again." The people laughed at this mightily; and to this
day I have heard it commended for rare.[50]

---

[47] Nash, I, 213.

[48] Morgan, p. 12, admits that it may be "merely a mistake," but
characteristically prefers to postulate an earlier version: "it might be
that he was reporting what took place in the old play."

[49] Cf. the allusion to "the red-nose innkeeper of Daventry" in *1
Henry IV*, IV, 2, 50, and Hemingway, p. 269. Cf. also Chambers
(1923), II, 107, 110, 112.

[50] From *Tarlton's Jests*, ed. Halliwell-Phillips, p. 24. Apparently
the three parts of the *Jests* were first published separately. The
second part was licensed on August 4, 1600 (Thomas Pavier) and

This passage, of course, substantiates my earlier statement that we possess positive knowledge of Tarlton's having acted in *The Famous Victories*.[51] And it is known that he died on September 3, 1588.[52] It is matter of record, besides, that one Rebecca, widow of one William Knell, remarried on March 10 of that year.[53] In all probability the actor was meant. One must suppose that he had died at least some months before Rebecca's new venture in matrimony. If so, the performance indicated cannot have taken place later than the winter of 1587–88; probability suggests the previous winter. And on other grounds, as I shall presently show, the earlier date seems likely.

---

the work (as a whole?) assigned to [Clement?] Knight from John Budge on February 21, 1609. The first known edition was printed in "London, by J. H., 1611." A unique copy of 1613 (title page reproduced herein) is in the Folger Shakespeare Library. The edition of 1638 uses the same impression with a different title page. Cf. Halliwell-Phillips (1844), p. 3.

[51] Nevertheless, there has been discussion of the question whether the passage from the *Jests* indicates that a different version of Scene 4 once existed. Daniel, p. vii, noted that "it was physically impossible for Tarlton to double the parts of Derick and the Chief Justice in a scene in which both appeared." But on the occasion cited, Derick's entrance could have been delayed until line 108, his preliminary bandying of words with the Chief Justice could have been sacrificed, and the parody with John deleted altogether. Such alteration of the text to meet the exigencies of the moment is commonplace in the theater. For Morgan, pp. 5, 11, the difficulty can only be solved by postulating a lost play with a double burlesque (on the analogy of *1 Henry IV*, II, 4) in which ultimately Derick (pretending to be the Chief Justice) was slapped by John (pretending to be the Prince). Also, Morgan supposes that Knell acted John, not the Prince as indicated in the *Jests*. This exemplifies only too well Morgan's unwillingness to read the evidence.

[52] Chambers (1923), II, 343.

[53] *Ibid.*, 327–28. Rebecca married John Heming, who collaborated with William Condell in editing Shakespeare's plays in the First Folio Edition of 1623.

To establish the date of the play's composition, the licensing of the Queen's men on November 28, 1583, would seem to provide a *terminus post quem*.[54] There is also the fact that the playwright almost certainly used John Stow's *Chronicles of England* (1580);[55] and he apparently did not know Holinshed in the edition of 1587.[56]

Certain topical references in the play can be shown apt for the months following the trial of Mary Stuart (October, 1586). Since they probably were added for a Court performance during that period—the Queen's played before Elizabeth on December 26, on January 1 and 6, and on February 28 in 1586–1587,[57]—the play may well have been written during the previous summer or fall.

3. Topical References

Every reader of *The Famous Victories* will have sensed the chauvinism of the play. Whether its patriotic fervor is less intense than that of Shakespeare's *Henry V* need not be argued—it is certainly less poetic and less effective. If, as I believe, the older play was written at a time when England had troops in the Low Countries against Spain and was bracing itself against invasion, the circumstances of the moment no doubt warranted a certain extravagance.

Less obviously, it appears that the play served as propa-

---

[54] *Ibid.*, 106.

[55] Lee, *DNB, s.v.*, "John Stow (1525?–1605)," reports an edition in 1584 which I have not found elsewhere indicated. See Explanatory Notes: Scene 2, lines 97–112.

[56] It can be shown that he used the edition of 1577; see App. A, Scene 9, n. 21. The amplified edition appeared in January, 1586–1587.

[57] Chambers (1923), II, 107.

ganda during the winter months of 1586–87, when Elizabeth was weighing the fate of Mary Stuart. Proof depends
upon the interpretation of a passage not hitherto commented
upon:

King. . . . Now, my lords, I will that my uncle, the Duke of York,
have the vanguard in the battle; the Earl of Derby, the Earl of Oxford, the Earl of Kent, the Earl of Nottingham, the Earl of Huntingdon I will have beside the army, that they may come fresh upon
them; and I myself, with the Duke of Bedford, the Duke of Clarence, and the Duke of Gloucester will be in the midst of the battle.
Furthermore, I will that my Lord of Willoughby and the Earl of
Northumberland, with their troops of horsemen, be continually
running like wings on both sides of the army—my Lord of Northumberland on the left wing. . . .

(Scene 14, lines 14–24)

That the King here delegates responsibilities rather specifically is clear enough; but unless one compares the passage with its source in Hall, the peculiar implications for
Elizabethans in the matter will not be apparent. This is what
Hall had written:

. . . he appointed a vanguard, of the which he made captain Edward
Duke of York who of a haughty courage had of the King required
and obtained that office: and with him were the lords Beaumond,
Willoughby and Fanhope, and this battle was all archers. The middle
guard was governed by the King himself with his brother the Duke
of Gloucester, and the Earls Marshal, Oxford and Suffolk, in which
were all the strong billmen. The Duke of Exeter, uncle to the King,
led the rear guard, which was mixed both with archers and billmen.
The horsemen like wings went on every side of the battle.

(Hall, f. HV, xvi, *verso*)

The dramatist's alterations are explicit and numerous. We
can only suppose that his purpose was definite.

First off, the new disposition of the sons of Henry IV
shows an almost pedantic concern for dramatic effect. The

King in the middle is attended by his brothers Bedford, Clarence, and Gloucester,[58] instead of by Gloucester and the two Earls Marshal; Hall had made it clear, however, that both Clarence and Bedford, stricken with the "flix" at Harfleur, had returned to England.[59] As in Hall, York, the King's cousin, holds the van, where he will gallantly die;[60] Exeter, the King's uncle, introduced earlier in the play as a courtier, is dropped,[61] together with all mention of the rear. The playwright has pretty much taken matters into his own hands.

Further modifications were designed to focus attention upon certain *Elizabethan* noblemen. To this end, the author omitted (besides Exeter) Beaumond, Fanhope, and Suffolk; all four names were extinct in the contemporary peerage. He retained from Hall (apart from royalty) only Oxford and Willoughby; great lords lived who bore these names.[62] He added Derby, Kent, Nottingham, Huntingdon, and Northumberland, quite unhistorical at Agincourt but immediately recognizable as Elizabethan personages.[63] It is

[58] John of Lancaster (1389–1435), Duke of Bedford; Thomas of Clarence (1388?–1421); Humphrey of Gloucester (1391–1447).

[59] Hall, f. HV, xiii, *verso*.

[60] Edward of Norwich (1373?–1415), 2nd Duke of York, the Aumerle (Albemarle) of Shakespeare's *Richard II*; cf. Hall, f. HV, xx, *recto*.

[61] Sir Thomas Beaufort (d. 1427) was not created Duke of Exeter until 1416; the playwright follows his source in allowing him the title earlier. On the reduction of his role in *The Famous Victories*, see below, n. 72.

[62] Edward de Vere (1550–1604), 17th Earl of Oxford; Peregrine Bertie (1555–1601), Lord Willoughby.

[63] Henry Stanley (1531–1593), 4th Earl of Derby; Henry Grey de Ruthin (d. 1615), 6th Earl of Kent; Charles, 2nd Lord Howard of Effingham (1536–1624), Earl of Nottingham as of 1596; Henry Hastings (1535–1595), 3d Earl of Huntingdon; Henry Percy (1564–1632), 9th Earl of Northumberland.

possible that the seven peers stood on the stage at a Court
performance to receive battle assignments from King
Henry; but perhaps the actors mimicked them. However
the matter was handled, reference to these seven contemporaries was certainly intended. Why?

Lord Oxford alone is a member of the *dramatis personae*.
He first appears in the play as an attendant upon Henry IV,
a role that the chronicles do not prescribe for Richard de
Vere (1385–1425), 11th Earl. Although Hall placed this
earlier Oxford in the "middle guard" at Agincourt, he says
nothing of his presenting to the King the report on the
opposing forces (Scene 14) and nothing of his having been
denied the van (Scene 12) and granted command of the famous maneuver for goring the French cavalry (Scene 14).
Such free alteration of received history first led B. M. Ward,
the biographer of Edward de Vere—he was not, by the way,
an "Oxfordian"—to claim that the elaborated role of Oxford
must be intended as complimentary to the Elizabethan
Earl.[64] And, in my opinion, he established the point.

Ward failed to produce a consistent idea of the Earl's
character, but it was not for want of documentation; he
assembled evidence that Oxford had been now the Queen's
lover, now quite out of her favor, now engaged in miscellaneous intrigue and feud, now a soldier, now active in minor
state affairs, etc. Moreover, to the question of why the playwright of *The Famous Victories* should have wished to cele-
brate Edward de Vere, he offered a plausible answer. In
1586 Oxford had returned from The Netherlands, having
had no great success in the campaigns, and, as usual, im-
poverished. On June 26 Elizabeth had granted him remark-

---

[64] Ward, *R.E.S.* (1928), p. 284. Ward does not, however, argue
the proposition in the biography.

able and substantial proof of her generosity and continuing esteem: an annual stipend of a thousand pounds.[65] She allowed no comparable personal grant through all the years of her reign. Pointing out that Oxford was not held publicly accountable for its expenditure, Ward proposed that the stipend was meant to assist him as theatrical entrepreneur for the Court, in such a way that it would not become known that the Queen was offering substantial backing to the acting companies:

> Elizabeth . . . was fully alive to the importance of masques and similar entertainments in promoting the well-being of the Court. A well-organized recreation department was as essential to herself and her courtiers as a plentifully supplied supper-table. There can be no doubt that a great part of the winter evening diversions during the early eighties emanated from Lord Oxford and John Lyly (who was in his service). She would very naturally be unwilling to allow so valuable a courtier to go bankrupt and be compelled to leave the Court just for lack of means to maintain his position.[66]

Others have gone beyond Ward to suggest, with some plausibility, that the funds were intended "for the first organized propaganda. Oxford was to produce plays which would educate the English people—most of whom could not read —in their country's history, in appreciation of its greatness, and of their own stake in its welfare." [67] In point of fact and time, a spate of chronicle plays did follow the authorization of the stipend. Is it not conceivable that they were produced with such subsidy? *The Famous Victories* may have

---

[65] Ward, *Seventeenth Earl*, p. 257. In 1928 Ward estimated this at $40,000.

[66] Ward, *Seventeenth Earl*, p. 282. Edmund Tilney, Master of Revels from 1579 to 1610, was allowed rather modest amounts at this time; cf. Chambers (1923), I, 90–91.

[67] The Ogburns, pp. 709–10, incorrectly attribute this idea to Ward.

been one of the first plays—perhaps the very first—commissioned for the Queen's men under this policy. If so, we should the better understand its patriotic zeal and its emphatic recommendation of an ancestor of Edward de Vere to the public.

In spite of the demonstration of the Queen's esteem and trust afforded by the warrant of June, 1586, there is reason to think that within a few months' time Lord Oxford was again in need of recommendation to her. For in October of that year occurred the momentous trial of Mary Stuart for treason against the Crown.[68] The Royal Commission, of which Oxford was a member, first sat at Fotheringay Castle; but when Elizabeth was persuaded of the likely outcome, she prorogued its meetings to London for her surveillance. After the unanimous verdict of guilt, she tried every device to postpone imposition of the penalty. On November 10, Oxford was appointed to a committee of the House of Lords to address the Queen on the subject of the sentence.[69] And she was continually harassed, the historian William Camden tells us, by courtiers, by "divers fiery-tongued preachers," and by "sundry also of the vulgar sort" who were eager to hasten Mary's death. Much of the time, "amidst sad-afflicting thoughts of mind . . . she delighted to be all alone, and to sit solitary by herself, neither looking up, nor uttering any speech." [70]

Certainly the Commissioners must have been given an intense display of the Queen's displeasure during the winter of 1586–87. We know, too, that there was some public resentment of their ruthlessness; a popular ballad of the time reviles

---

[68] For a brief summary, cf. Black, pp. 331–35.
[69] Ward, *Seventeenth Earl*, p. 351.
[70] Camden, III, 199.

them.[71] They may well have wished to vindicate themselves as patriots both in public and at Court. Oxford, Derby, Kent, and "Nottingham," who were all members of the Commission, may have asked the assistance of the actors, or it may have been voluntarily offered. The playwright, perhaps already at work on his piece of nationalistic propaganda, may have been instructed to introduce Oxford into the *dramatis personae* [72] and to insert the names of the others ostentatiously. For good measure, and not unaccountably, Huntingdon, Willoughby, and Northumberland were added to the group, though these peers had not sat on the Commission.

Lord Oxford, recently the recipient of unusual favor from the Queen, presumably had not hesitated to address her, as a representative of the Lords' committee and to argue in favor of Mary's execution. Himself a lapsed Catholic (having reverted to Anglicanism in 1581),[73] he was quite without sympathy for the Scottish Queen. Elizabeth preferred compromise in religious matters.

Henry Stanley, 4th Earl of Derby, had frequently served as Commissioner for Ecclesiastical Causes. He had punished

---

[71] Halliwell-Phillips (1845), XV, 38.

[72] Oxford gradually usurps Exeter's position as attendant upon the King. That his role was an afterthought is suggested by two stage directions: *Enter Henry the Fourth, with the Earl of Exeter, and the Lord of Oxford* (Scene 3), and *Enter Lord[s] of Exeter and Oxford* (Scene 8). I take it that in the first instance *and the Lord of Oxford* and in the second *and Oxford* were added to the original. Exeter does not speak in Scene 5; in Scene 8 he speaks three times in unison with Oxford; only in Scene 9 does he have a separate entrance. The speech allotted him by the chronicles is, however, deleted. Thereafter he is omitted, and he is dropped from the ordering of the battle (see above, p. 184). Oxford, in contrast, speaks in Scenes 3, 5, 8, 9, 12, 14, and 15.

[73] Ward, *Seventeenth Earl*, pp. 206, 214.

recusants in Lancashire [74] but, in general, had a reputation for fairness and had been trusted by Elizabeth.[75] She was probably disappointed in him, but the players would have defended him, it may be supposed, if only because the Derbys had supported acting companies since the time of Henry VIII.[76] He was head of the wealthiest family in England.

Henry Grey de Ruthin, 6th Earl of Kent, had first responsibility for the details of the execution.[77] At the trial he plied Mary with argument in an effort to confute her opinions, and at the execution he told her, "Your life will be your death; and your death the life of our Religion." When the Dean of Peterborough cried, "So perish all enemies of Queen Elizabeth!", Kent was first to say "Amen!" [78] This nobleman may have had some connection with the theater, for in the "Show of the Coronation," which was incorporated in Dr. Thomas Legge's *Richardus Tertius*,[79] he had carried a naked sword, enacting with others an anachronistic role. Two of his associates on that occasion had been the Earls of Derby and Huntingdon.[80]

Charles, 2nd Lord Howard of Effingham, was created Earl of Nottingham on October 22, 1596; the 1598 text of

---

[74] Pollard, *DNB, s.v.,* "Henry Stanley (1531–1593)."

[75] Froude, XII, 327.

[76] Chambers (1923), II, 118 ff.

[77] Froude, XII, 328, 331.

[78] Camden, III, 205. According to Froude, XII, 351, Kent was "an austere Puritan to whom she [Mary] was merely a wicked woman overtaken at last by the punishment she had too long deserved and escaped."

[79] Written presumably in 1579; the list of actors probably dates from March, 1580. Cf. Chambers (1923), III, 408, and, for the "Show of the Coronation," Field, p. 126.

[80] A third was Henry Percy (1532?–1585), 8th Earl of Northumberland; see below, n. 89.

The Famous Victories gives him the benefit of his later title.[81] Howard shared with Oxford an enthusiastic interest in the theater and for many years (1576–1604) was patron of a company. He had been Lord Chamberlain at Court from 1583 to 1585, in charge of the Revels. Thereafter his company frequently played before the Queen.[82] In the winter of 1586–87, when Howard had become Lord High Admiral of England, it was apparently he who most persuasively argued with Elizabeth that Mary should be put to death.[83]

Oxford, Derby, Kent, and "Nottingham" thus shared special responsibility for the death of Mary. The other peers likewise won their places at the dramatic Agincourt for involvement in the issues of the day.

Henry Hastings, 3d Earl of Huntingdon, had much at stake while Mary's fate was being determined. It is possible that he had been quite deliberately excluded from the Commission, for, by virtue of a devious claim, he had long considered himself heir apparent and, as such, Mary's rival.[84] He had been briefly a custodian of Mary in 1569.

---

[81] "Effingham" probably stood in the original for "Nottingham" in Scene 14, line 16.

[82] Chambers (1923), II, 134–35.

[83] Froude, XI, 343: "Lord Howard of Effingham, not at all the most extreme of Elizabeth's advisers, came to her (February 1, 1587) to represent that the condition of the country could no longer be trifled with; that some positive course must be taken with the Queen of Scots. He himself, like every other intelligent statesman who was not a traitor at heart, had long decided that she ought to be executed. For the first time Elizabeth appeared really shaken. The long suspension of the sentence made it doubly difficult to enforce, but she desired Howard to tell Davison, who in Walsingham's absence was acting as sole secretary, to come to her, and to bring the warrant with him."

[84] Cf. Black, p. 78, and Henderson, *DNB*, *s.v.*, "Henry Hastings (1535–1595)."

Peregrine Bertie, Lord Willoughby as of 1580, came of a strongly Protestant family; in 1577, Oxford seems to have opposed his marriage to his sister, Lady Mary Vere, on that ground.[85] Nevertheless, after Oxford's rejection of Catholicism, he and his brother-in-law were on terms of close friendship. At the time of Mary's trial and execution, Willoughby was rendering brilliant service in the Low Countries.[86] A broadside ballad survives to witness his public acclaim.[87] Though no courtier,[88] Willoughby must have stood high in the Queen's favor in 1586–87; and all six of the other "heroes" at Agincourt in the months after Mary's condemnation would have benefitted by association with his name.

This would have been particularly true of Northumberland, whose reputation was, at the time, clouded. The reference is undoubtedly to Henry Percy, the 9th Earl, whose father had, on June 21, 1585, met a mysterious death in the Tower, where he had been imprisoned for treason as an active supporter of Throckmorton in the Catholic cause.[89] Mary had evidently expected the young Earl's allegiance, for in her second letter to Babington, crucial evidence at the

---

[85] Ward, *Seventeenth Earl*, p. 230.

[86] Lee, *DNB*, s.v., "Peregrine Bertie (1555–1601)."

[87] "Brave Lord Willoughby" in *Roxburghe Ballads*, IV, 8.

[88] According to Sir Robert Naunton, *Fragmenta Regalia* (1641), cited by Ward, *Seventeenth Earl*, p. 151: "My Lord Willoughby was one of the Queen's best swordsmen. . . . I have heard it spoken that had he not slighted the Court, but applied himself to the Queen, he might have enjoyed a plentiful portion of her grace; and it was his saying—and it did him no good—that he was none of the Reptilia: intimating that he could not creep on the ground, and that the Court was not his element. For, indeed, as he was a great soldier, so he was of amiable magnanimity, and could not brook the obsequiousness and assiduity of the Court."

[89] Lee, *DNB*, s.v., "Henry Percy (1532?–1585)."

trial, she had expressed the hope of enlisting him in her behalf.[90] Since December, 1585, however, Northumberland had been in Holland in the service of the Crown. In *The Famous Victories*, his name is twice linked with Willoughby's.[91]

Our consideration of the seven Elizabethan noblemen—Oxford, Derby, Kent, Nottingham, Huntingdon, Willoughby, and Northumberland—has related six to the fate of Mary Stuart.[92] Of Willoughby's ardent Protestantism there can be no question. It is quite safe, therefore, to assert the topicality of these references during (or shortly after) the winter of 1586–87. That this coincides with other evidence as to the date of composition and production of the play in its earliest form has already been pointed out.

I have indicated that in this period the Queen's men played at Court four times: December 26, January 1 and 6, and February 28. Since the execution of Mary on February 8 may well have lessened tensions there, and since the Queen could hardly have tolerated so obvious (and even facetious) a plea for her favor earlier, February 28 was, it appears, the

---

90 *Ibid.*, "Henry Percy (1564–1632)."

91 Scene 13, lines 20–21; also 14, 21–22. George Peele, himself a playwright for the Queen's Company, in his *Honor of the Garter* (1593), salutes the "Wizard Earl" as: "Renowned Lord, Northumberland's fair flower,/The Muses' love, patron and favorite,/That artisans and scholars dost embrace. . . ."

92 There is also negative evidence to prove the topicality of such references. Ralph Neville (1364–1425), 1st Earl of Westmorland, who, by the testimony of the chronicles, had played a part in the deliberations prior to the declaration of war against France, is excluded in Scene 9 of *The Famous Victories*, almost certainly because his Elizabethan descendant, Charles Neville, 6th Earl, was in exile abroad after his notorious attempt in 1569 to release Mary Stuart from captivity; cf. Hall, f. HV, v, *recto*, and Archbold, *DNB, s.v.*, "Charles Neville (1543–1601)."

precise date of the Court performance of *The Famous Victories*. The performance at the Bull at Bishopsgate, recorded in *Tarlton's Jests*, probably occurred at about the same time.

It may have been Tarlton who first urged upon the playwright the device of elaborating the role of the medieval Oxford to serve the cause of Edward de Vere, and who proposed the other topical references. (If so, when Marlowe in his Prologue to *Tamburlaine* [*c.* 1587] complained of "such conceits as clownage keeps in pay," he may have been glancing at both Tarlton and the anonymous author of *The Famous Victories*.) We know, at any rate, that Tarlton was sometimes sought out by noblemen whose affairs at Court were unsteady. And it is testified by sober Dr. Fuller that he understood the Queen's moods and knew how to influence her opinions:

When Queen Elizabeth was serious, I dare not say sullen, and out of good humour, he could un-dumpish her at his pleasure. Her highest favorites would, in some cases, go to Tarlton before they would go to the Queen, and he was their usher to prepare their advantageous access unto her. In a word, he told the Queen more of her faults than most of her chaplains, and cured her melancholy better than all of her physicians.[93]

It will be remembered that in recent years there has been some expense of spirit and considerable waste of time in the effort to identify Shakespeare with Lord Oxford.[94] An attempt has also been made, one way or another, to associate him with the House of Derby.[95] I must acknowledge in-

---

[93] Fuller, III, 140.

[94] Cf. the Ogburns, *passim*. On Ward's notion that Oxford may have written *The Famous Victories*, see Explanatory Notes: Scene 4, lines 21–23.

[95] Keen and Lubbock, *passim*.

debtedness to these investigations for two pieces of evidence that have bearing upon the present argument. Shakespeare, they have conclusively shown, has, in canonical plays, undertaken to compliment both Oxford and Derby, by the methods used in *The Famous Victories*. Thus, in *3 Henry VI* he has extensively elaborated the role of John de Vere (1443–1513), the 13th Earl. In his dramatic version, De Vere is lauded as a staunch Lancastrian; he accompanies Queen Margaret and Prince Edward in their exile in France and appears before Louis XI in 1462 to enlist aid for them. Actually, according to Hall, John de Vere accepted the Yorkist Edward VI as king until 1470.[96] Again, in *Richard III*, the same de Vere is displayed as an ardent supporter of Richmond at Bosworth Field.[97] To have been a good Lancastrian implied, in Tudor times, unimpeachable loyalty to the throne. There can thus be no doubt that Shakespeare himself, with special purpose, emphasized the services of Oxford in *3 Henry VI* and *Richard III*.[98]

The attempt to prove Shakespeare's close association with the Derbys has also brought out the fact that in *Richard III* he elaborates the historical role of Thomas Stanley (1435?–1504), often calling him Earl of Derby in anticipation of his achieving that title after Bosworth.[99] Other Stanleys are fitfully introduced in *2* and *3 Henry VI*. The playwright's procedure in these cases is similar to that used in his treatment of John de Vere in *3 Henry VI* and *Richard III*. And in these instances, I insist, the method is identical with that used by the playwright of *The Famous Victories*.

---

[96] Hall, f. HVI, xxxi, *verso*.

[97] Cf. the Ogburns, pp. 321 ff.

[98] This development also appears in *The True Tragedy of Richard III*, pp. 31, 53–57, 67.

[99] Keen and Lubbock, pp. 83 ff.

It should also be noted that the Queen's Men acted in private theatricals before the 4th Earl at Lathom House on October 10, 1588, and again at Knowsley in June, 1590. In 1592, the company of Ferdinando Stanley, Lord Strange, Derby's eldest son, produced "Harey the vj," in all probability Shakespeare's *1 Henry VI*.[100] It has been proposed that when Oxford's daughter, Lady Elizabeth Vere, married Derby's second son, William, in 1595, the occasion was marked by the first performance of *A Midsummer Night's Dream*.[101]

4. SUMMARY

The evidence considered in this chapter suggests only that Shakespeare's authorship of *The Famous Victories* is reasonably presumptive. The single document which might be held to substantiate the theory, James' letter to Bourchier, does not certainly refer to this play, for Derick—not Oldcastle—is its buffoon. We must suppose either that James did not have *The Famous Victories* in mind and believed another play to have been "Shakespeare's first show of Henry the Fifth," or that he intended reference to our play but was inaccurate about Oldcastle. It is difficult to choose between these alternatives.

More reliable as evidence, I believe, is the fact that the aggrandizement of Oxford's role in *The Famous Victories* parallels in method the treatment of Oxford in *3 Henry VI* and *Richard III*, and of Derby in *Richard III*. I believe this

---

[100] Chambers (1923), II, 118 ff.
[101] Chambers (1930), I, 358.

means that Shakespeare was repeating a device he had previously used.

Support to the theory of Shakespearean authorship is given by the fact that the play was first printed by Thomas Creed, of all Elizabethan stationers the most alert to Shakespeare's marketability; he printed it in the year which marks Shakespeare's attainment of general notoriety.

That it was certainly a Queen's play, written in 1586, also lends probability to my thesis; Shakespeare may very well have begun his work in London at about that time, and his association with the Queen's is at any rate traditional. That, by the statement of Alsop's title page, the play was later in the repertory of the King's Majesty's Servants, confirms its association with Shakespeare's own company. It may or may not be significant for this argument that it was reprinted the year after the dramatist's death.

Tarlton acted in the play, and this is consistent with the belief that Shakespeare was early associated with him. The eighteenth-century subscription to the engraving of Tarlton, though of uncertain origin, offers some further substantiation.

All in all, it seems to me fair to claim that the external data and documentary evidence strengthen the likelihood of Shakespeare's authorship of *The Famous Victories*. They therefore reinforce the argument of the earlier chapters of this book.

APPENDICES

¶ *King Henry of Monmouth.*

Anno reg. I.
Titus Liuius.

Enrie the fifth began his raigne y̆ .xx.day of March in y̆ yere.1412.This Prince exceeded the mean stature of men, he was beautiful of visage, his necke long , bodye slender and leane , and hys bones smal: neuertheleste he was of maruellous greate strength, and passing swifte in running, in so much that he with two other of his Lords without bow oꝛ other engine, woulde take a wilde Buck oꝛ Doe in a large Park: he delighted in sōgs & musical instrumēts, in so much y̆ in his chappel amōgst other his pꝛiuate pꝛayers, he vsed certaine Psalmes of Dauid translated into heroycall *English* mæter, by Iohn Lydgate , Monke of *Bury*.

Whilst his father liued, beyng accōpanyed w̃ some of his yong

A Page from John Stow, *The Chronicles of England* (1580)

Reproduced by permission of The Folger Shakespeare Library.

In Sh:

pursuivants = attendants

Zounds = God's wounds.
        (Gog's wounds)

bots = a disease of horses

dumps = dumps = melancholy

Harfleur siege = Aug, 1415.

Kings meet May 20, 1420

    and June 3, 1420

        at Troyes

check p 233 in
    dk. blue text
        after writing about
            action.

APPENDIX A

Sources *

Sir Thomas Elyot, *The Book of the Governor* (1531).
Edward Hall, *The Union of the Two Noble and Illustrious Families of Lancaster and York* (1550).
Raphael Holinshed, *The Chronicles of England, Scotland, and Ireland* (1577).
John Stow, *The Chronicles of England, from Brute unto this present year of Christ* (1580).

Scene i

STOW, pp. 582–83.

Henry [1] the fifth began his reign the 20th day of March in the year 1412. This prince exceeded the mean stature of men. He was beautiful of visage, his neck long, body slender and lean, and his bones small; nevertheless, he was of marvel-

---

* Footnotes will be found at the end of this Appendix.

ous great strength, and passing swift in running, insomuch that he with two other of his lords without bow or other engine,[2] would take a wild buck or doe in a large park. He delighted in songs and musical instruments, insomuch that in his chapel amongst other his[3] private papers, he used[4] certain Psalms of David translated into heroical English meter by John Lydgate, Monk of Bury.[5]

Whilst his father lived, being accompanied with some of his young lords and gentlemen, he would wait in disguised array for his own receivers, and distress[6] them of their money. And sometimes at such enterprises both he and his company were surely beaten. And when his receivers made to him their complaints, how they were robbed in their coming unto him, he would give them discharge of so much money as they had lost. And besides that they should not depart from him without great rewards for their trouble and vexation; especially they should be rewarded that had best resisted him and his company, and of whom he had received the greatest and most strokes. But after the decease of his father there was never any youth[7] or wildness that might have place in him, but all his acts were suddenly changed into gravity and discretion.[8]

SCENES 2 AND 3

STOW, p. 573.

Upon the eve of St. John Baptist [1410] the King's son being in Eastcheap at supper, after midnight betwixt two or three of the clock, a great debate[1] happened between his men and men of the Court, lasting an hour till the Mayor and Sheriffs with other citizens ceased the same, for the which the said Mayor, Sheriffs and twelve Aldermen were sent after by writ to appear before the King there for to answer;

at which the King with his sons, and divers other lords, were highly moved against the city. William Gascoigne, Chief Justice, inquired of the Mayor and the Aldermen, for the citizens, whether they would put them in the King's grace.[2] Whereunto they answered, they had not offended the King nor his sons, but according to law staunched the debates. Then the King seeing it would be none otherwise, forgave altogether, and they departed.[3]

SCENE 4

ELYOT, f. 122, *recto*–123, *recto*.

The most renowned prince King Henry the Fifth, late king of England, during the life of his father was noted to be fierce and of wanton courage. It happened that one of his servants, whom he well favored, for felony by him committed was arraigned at the King's Bench: whereof he, being advertised [1] and incensed by light persons about him, in furious rage came hastily to the bar where his servant stood as a prisoner, and commanded him to be ungyved and set at liberty: whereat all men were abashed, reserved [2] the Chief Justice, who humbly exhorted the Prince to be contented, that his servant might be ordered according to the ancient laws of this realm, or if he would have him saved from the rigor of the laws, that he should obtain, if he might, of the King his father his gracious pardon: whereby no law or justice should be derogate. With which answer the Prince, nothing appeased but rather more inflamed, endeavored himself to take away his servant. The Judge, considering the perilous example and inconvenience [3] that might thereby ensue, with a valiant spirit and courage, commanded the Prince upon his allegiance to leave the prisoner and depart his way. With which commandment the Prince being set all in a fury, all chafed and in a terrible manner, came up to the place of judgement, men thinking that he would have slain the Judge, or have done him some damage. But the Judge sitting still without moving, declaring the majesty of the King's place of judgement, and with an assured and bold countenance, had to the Prince these words following: "Sir, remember yourself. I keep here the place of the King your sovereign lord and father, to whom you owe double obedience. Wherefore eftsoons [4] in his name, I charge you desist of your willfulness and unlawful enterprise. And from henceforth give good example to those which hereafter shall be your proper subjects. And now for your contempt and disobedience, go you to the prison of the King's Bench, whereunto I commit you. And remain you there prisoner until the pleasure of the King your father be further known." With which words being abashed, and also wondering at the marvelous gravity of that worshipful Justice, the noble Prince, laying his weapon apart, doing reverence [5] departed and went to the King's Bench, as he was commanded: whereat his servants, disdaining, came and showed to the King all the whole affair: whereat he awhiles studying, after [6] as a man all ravished with gladness, holding his eyes and hands up toward heaven, abrayed,[7] saying with a loud voice, "O merciful God, how much am I above all other men bound to your infinite goodness; specially for that you have given me a judge who feareth not to minister justice! And also a son who can suffer semblably [8] and obey justice!"

Now here a man may behold three persons worthy excellent memory: first, a judge who, being a subject, feared not to execute justice on the eldest son of his sovereign lord, and by the order of nature his successor. Also a prince and son and heir of the King, [who], in the midst of his fury, most [9]

considered his evil example and the judge's constancy in
justice, than his own estate or willful appetite. Thirdly, a
noble King and a wise father, who contrary to the custom
of parents, rejoiced to see his son and the heir of his crown,
to be for his disobedience by his subject corrected.

Wherefore I conclude that nothing is more honorable, or
to be desired in a prince or noble man, than placability.[10] As
contrarywise, nothing is so detestable or to be feared in such
a one as wrath and cruel malignity.

HALL, f. HV, i, *recto*.
For imprisonment of one of his wanton mates and unthrifty playfairs[11] he struck the Chief Justice with his fist
on the face. For which offense he was not only committed
to strait prison, but also by his father put out of the Privy
Council and banished the Court.

Cf. also **Holinshed, p. 1165b.**

SCENES 5 AND 6

STOW, pp. 576–78.
. . . he [Henry IV] was taken with sickness, of the
which he languished till his appointed hour, during which
sickness some evilly disposed people labored to make dissension between the King and the Prince his son, by reason
whereof, and by the act[1] of youth, which he exercised more
than meanly,[2] and for the great recourse of people unto him,
of whom his court was at all times more abundant than
[that of] the King his father, the King suspected that he
would presume to usurp the crown, he being alive: which
suspicious jealousy was occasion that he in part withdrew

his affection and singular love from the Prince. But when this noble Prince was advertised[3] of his father's jealousy, he disguised[4] himself in a gown of blue satin, made full of small eyelets, and at every eyelet the needle wherewith it was made hanging still by a thread of silk. . . . Thus appareled, with a great company of lords and other noblemen of his court, he came to the King his father, who at that time lay at Westminster, where at his coming (by his own commandment) not one of his company advanced himself further than the fire in the hall, notwithstanding that they were greatly and oft desired to the contrary by the lords and great estates[5] of the King's Court. And that the Prince had commanded, to give the less occasion of mistrust to the King his father, but he himself only accompanied by the King's house[6] passed forth to the King his father, to whom after due salutation he desired to show the intent of his mind in secret manner. Then the King caused himself to be borne in his chair into his secret chamber (because he was desired and might not go[7]), where in the presence of three or four persons, in whom the King had most confidence, he commanded the Prince to show the effect of his mind. Then the Prince kneeling down before his father, said to him these words, "Most redoubted[8] Lord and father, I am this time come to your presence as your liegeman, and as your natural son, in all things to obey your Grace as my sovereign Lord and father. And whereas I understand you have me suspect of my behavior against your Grace, and that you fear I would usurp your crown against the pleasure of your Highness, from my conversation[9] your Grace knoweth that if you were in fear of any man, of what estate soever he were, my duty were to the endangering of my life to punish that person, thereby to raze that sore from your heart. And then how much rather ought I to suffer death to bring your Grace from the fear that you have of me that am your natural son and your liegeman. And to that intent I have this day by confession and receiving the sacrament, prepared myself, and therefore most redoubted Lord and father, I beseech you in the honor of God, for the easing of your heart, here before your knees to slay me with this dagger." And at that word with all reverence he delivered to the King his dagger, saying, "My Lord and father, my life is not so desirous[10] to me that I would live one day that should be to your displeasure, nor I covet not so much my life as I do your pleasure and welfare, and in your thus doing,[11] here in the presence of these lords and before God at the day of judgement, I clearly forgive you my death." At these words of the Prince, the King, taken with compassion of heart, cast from him the dagger, and embracing the Prince kissed him, and with effusion of tears said unto him, "My right dear and heartily beloved son, it is true that I had you partly suspect, and as I now perceive, undeserved on your part. But seeing this your humility and faithfulness, I shall neither slay you, nor from henceforth have you any more in mistrust, for no[12] report that shall be made to me, and thereof I assure you upon mine honor." Thus by his great wisdom was the wrongful imagination of his father's hate utterly avoided, and himself restored to the King's former grace and favor.

Cf. also **Holinshed, pp. 1159a–60b.**

HALL, f. HIV, xxxii.

After these great and fortunate chances[13] happened to King Henry, he, perfectly remembering that there could be no more praise given to a prince than to execute his office in administering justice . . .

After he had appeased all civil dissensions he showed himself so gently to all men that he got him more love of his nobles in his latter days than he had malice and ill will of them in the beginning.

. . . he was taken with a sore, sudden disease and laid in his bed, which disease was no leprosy stricken by the hands of God as foolish friars before declared, for then [14] he neither would for shame, nor for debility was able to enterprise [15] so great a journey as [he had planned] into Jewry in his own person, but he was taken with a sore apoplexy of the which he languished until his appointed hour, and had none other grief nor malady.

SCENE 8

HALL, f. HIV, xxxii, *verso*.

During his sickness, as authors write, he [Henry IV] caused his crown to be set on the pillow at his bed's head and suddenly his pang so sore troubled him that he lay as though all his vital spirits had been from him departed. Such chamberlains as had the cure [1] and charge of his body, thinking him to be departed and dead, covered his face with a linen cloth. The Prince his son being thereof advertised [2] entered into the chamber and took away the crown and departed. The father being suddenly revived out of his trance quickly perceived the lack of his crown, and having knowledge that the Prince his son had possessed it, caused him to repair to his presence, requiring of him for what cause he had so misused himself. [3] The Prince with a good

Anno. 1.
Henry
the .5.

1413

being proclaymed King, by the name of Henry the fifth, in the yeare of the world. 5375. after the birth of our Sauior. 1413. the third, or thereabouts, of the Emperor Sigismond, the three and thirtie of Charles the sixt king of Fraunce, and about the sixth of James the first K. of Scotland.

Homage done to king Henry before his coronation.

Suche greate hope, and good expectation was hadde of thys mans fortunate successe to followe; that within three dayes after hys fathers deceasse, diuers noble men, and honourable personages, did to him homage, and sware to him due obedience, which had not bin seen done to any of his predecessors kings of this Realm, till they hadde bin possessed of the Crowne, and receyued their oth well and truely to gouerne.

The day of K. Henryes coronation a very tempestuous daye.

He was Crowned the ninth of Aprill, beeyng Passion Sonday, which was a sore, ruggie and intemperate daye, with wind, snow and sleete, that men greatly marueiled thereat, making diuers interpretations, what the same mighte signifie.

H EARE Prince of Wales, sonne and heire to Kyng Henrye the fourth, borne at Monmouth in wales, on the ryuer of Wye, after his father was departed this life, toke vpon him the regimente of thys Realme of Englande, the twentith of Marche.

A notable example of a worthy Prince.

But what so euer mens fancies bereof might coniecture, this King was the man, that according to the olde prouerbe, declared and shewed in what sort honors ought to change maners, for immediately after that hee was inuested Kyng, and had receyued the Crowne, hee determined with him selfe to putte vppon him the shape of a new man, turning insolencie and wildnesse into grauitie and sobernesse: And whereas hee hadde passed his youth in wanton pastime, and riotous misorder, with a sort of misgouerned mates, and vnthriftie playfeers, hee nowe banished them from his presence (not vnrewarded, nor yet preferred) inhibiting them vppon a great payne, not once to approche, lodge, or soiourne within tenne miles of his Court of mansion: and in their places he electd and chose men of grauitie, witte, and high policie, by whose wise counsell,

and prudent aduertisement, he might at al times rule to his honoure, and gouerne to his prosper; whereas if he should haue retayned the other idle companions aboute him, he doubted least they might haue allured him vnto suche lewd and light partes, as with them before tyme he had youthfully vsed, not alwayes to his owne commendation, nor yet to the contentation of his father, in so much, that where on a time, hee stroke the chiefe iustice on the face with his fist, for imprisoning one of his mates, he was not only committed to straighte prison himselfe by the sayde chiefe Iustice, but also of his father putte out of the priuie counsell, and banished the Court, and his brother Thomas Duke of Clarence electd president of the Counsell, to his great displeasure and open reproch: but nowe that hee was once placed in the royall throne, and regall seate of the audacity answered, "Sir, to mine and all men's judgements you seemed dead in this world, wherefore I as your next and apparent heir took that as mine own and not as yours." [4] "Well, fair son," said the King with a great sigh, "what right I had to it and how I enjoyed it God knoweth!" "Well," saith the Prince, "if you die king I will have the garland [5] and trust to keep it with the sword against all mine enemies as you have done." "Well," said the King, "I commit all to God. And remember you to do well." And with that [he] turned himself in his bed and shortly after departed to God, in a chamber of the Abbot of Westminster called Jerusalem the 20th day of March in the year of our Lord 1413 and in the year of his age 46, when he had reigned thirteen years, five months and odd days in much perplexity and little pleasure.

Cf. also **Holinshed, pp. 1162a–b.**

SCENE 9

STOW, pp. 583–84.

The ninth day of April (1413) he [Henry V] was crowned at Westminster, by Thomas Arundel, Archbishop of Canterbury, after which coronation he called unto him all those young lords and gentlemen that were the followers of his young acts, to every one of whom he gave rich and bounteous gifts, and then commanded that as many as would change their manners as he intended to do should abide with him in his court, and to all that would persevere in their former light conversation, he gave express commandment upon pain of their heads never after that day to come in his presence.

HALL, f. HV, i, *recto*.

This king, this man was he, which (according to the old proverb) declared and showed that honors ought to change manners, for incontinent after he was installed in the siege royal, and had received the crown and scepter of the famous and fortunate region, determined with himself to put on the shape of a new man, and use another sort of living, turning insolency and wildness into gravity and soberness, and wavering vice into constant virtue. And to the intent that he would so continue without going back, and not thereunto be allured by his familiar companions, with whom he had passed his young age amid wanton pastime and riotous misorder . . . he therefore banished and separated from him all his old flatterers and familiar companions (not unrewarded nor yet unpreferred), inhibiting[1] them upon a great pain not once to approach either to his speech or presence, nor yet to lodge or sojourn within ten miles of his court or mansion. And in their places he elected and chose men of gravity, men of wit, and men of high policy, by whose wise counsel and prudent instruction he might at all times rule to his honor and govern to his profit. This prince was almost the Arabical Phoenix, and amongst his predecessors a very paragon, for that he, amongst all governors, chiefly did remember that a king ought to be ruler with wit, gravity, circumspection, diligence, and constancy, and for that cause to have a rule to him committed, not for an honor, but for an onerous charge and daily burden, and not to look so much on other men's livings as to consider and remember his own doings and proper acts.

STOW, p. 584.

Sir John Oldcastle, at that time Lord of Cobham, for divers points touching the sacrament, before the Archbishop of Canterbury, and the Bishops of London, Winchester, and others, was convicted and committed to the Tower of London, out of which he broke over the walls in the night and escaped.

HALL, f. HV, ii, *verso.*

During this first year, Sir John Oldcastle, which by [2] his wife was called Lord Cobham, a valiant captain and an hardy gentleman, was accused to the Archbishop of Canterbury of certain points of heresy, which bishop, knowing him to be highly in the King's favor, declared to his Highness the whole accusation.

STOW, pp. 586–87.

To this parliament (1414) came the Ambassadors of the French King, and also of the Duke of Burgundy, but not with like intent and purpose, for the Duke of Burgundy desired aid against the Duke of Orleans, promising (as men said) more than he was able to perform, wherefore the King of England sent solemn ambassadors to them both, amongst whom were the Bishops of Durham and Norwich as chief: these were ofttimes sent into France, and the French King's ambassadors were sent hither, with great cost on both sides, but no hope of peace to be had.[3] . . . Our ambassadors, the Bishops of Durham and Norwich, returning now the second time out of France, declared to the King, that the Frenchmen did but use fraud and deceits; wherefore the King being stirred up unto anger, determined to abate their scornings, and to teach them to understand their folly, in awaking a sleeping dog. And forthwith the King commanded all the prelates and nobles of the realm to come to London, there to intreat of [4] weighty matters concerning the realm.

HALL, ff. HV, iii, *verso–x, verso.*

On a day when the King was present in the parliament, Henry Chicheley, Archbishop of Canterbury, thereto newly preferred,[5] which beforetime had been a monk of the Carthusians, a man which had professed wilful[6] poverty in religion and yet coming abroad much desired honor, and a man much regarding God's law, but more loving his own lucre, [spoke as follows]: ". . . Regard well, my sovereign Lord, your just and true title to the realm of France, by God's law and man's law to you lawfully divoluted,[7] as very heir to Queen Isabel,[8] your great grandmother, daughter to King Philip the Fair[9] and sister and heir to three kings deceasing without issue. This inheritance from the woman is declared to be just by the Mosaical law[10] and used and approved by the Gallican descent,[11] as I have before declared. Therefore, for God's sake, lease not your patrimony, disinherit not your heirs, dishonor not yourself, diminish not your title, which your noble progenitors have so highly esteemed. Advance forth your banner, fight for your right, conquer your inheritance, spare not sword, blood, or fire. Your war is just, your cause is good, and your claim true. Therefore, courageously set forward your war against your enemies. . . ." When the Archbishop had finished his prepared purpose, Ralph, Earl of Westmorland, a man of no less gravity than experience, and of no more experience than stomach . . . rose up, and making his obeisance to the King said: ". . . My counsel is, first to invade Scotland, and by God's grace to conquer and join that region to your empire, and to restore the renowned monarchy of Britain to her old estate and preeminence, and so beautified with realms and furnished with people, to enter into France for the recovering of your righteous title and true inheritance, in observing the old ancient proverb used by our forefathers, which saith, *He that will France win, must with Scotland first begin."* "No," saith the Duke of Exeter, uncle to the King, who was well learned, and [had been] sent into Italy by his father intending to have been a priest, *"He that will Scotland win, let him with France first begin.* . . . And because the Lord of Westmorland hath alleged that the Romans desired the dominion of such as were under flight of their own eagle, or whose possessions were a mote to their eye, . . . behold the conditions [12] of the councillors and the desires of the movers! [13] What persons were they which coveted their poor neighbors rather than rich foreigners? Men effeminate, more meet for a carpet than a camp, men of weak stomach desiring rather to walk in a pleasant garden than pass the seas in a tempestuous storm." . . . The King, like a wise prince and politic governor, intending to observe the ancient orders of famous kings and renowned potentates, used as well among pagans as Christians, which is, not to invade another man's territory without open war and the cause of the same to him published and declared, dispatched into France his uncle the Duke of Exeter and the Earl of Dorset. . . . The English ambassadors according to their commission required of the French King [14] to deliver to the King of England the realm and crown of France with the entire Duchies of Aquitaine, Normandy and Anjou, with the countries of Poitieu and Maine and divers other requests, offering that if the French King would without war or effusion of Christian blood render to the King their master his very right and lawful inheritance, that he would be content to take in marriage the Lady Katherine, [15] daughter to the French King, and to endow her with all the duchies and countries before rehearsed. The Frenchmen were much abashed at these demands thinking them very unreasonable and far excessive, and yet not willing to make any determinate answer till they had farther breathed in so weighty a cause, prayed the English ambassadors to say to the King their master that they now having no opportunity to conclude in so high a matter would shortly send ambassadors into England who should certify and declare to the king their whole mind, purpose and answer. The English ambassadors, nothing content with this doing, departed into England making relation of everything that was said or done. Here I overpass how some writers say that the Dolphin, thinking King Henry to be given still to such plays and light follies as he exercised and used before the time that he was exalted to the crown sent to him a tun of tennis balls to play with, as who said that he could better manage tennis than war, and was more expert in light games than martial policy. Whether he were moved with this unwise present, or, espying that the Frenchmen dallied and vainly delayed his purpose and demand, was moved and pricked forward, I cannot judge, but sure it is that after the return of his ambassadors, he being of a haughty courage and bold stomach, living now in the pleasantest time of his age,[16] much desiring to enlarge and dilate his empire and dominion, determined fully to make war in France, conceiving a good trust and perfect hope in this point which he had before experimented,[17] which is, that victory for the most part followeth where right leadeth, advanced forward by justice and set forth by equity. . . . The ambassadors[18] accompanied with 350 horses, passed the sea at Calais and landed at Dover, before whose arrival the King was departed from Windsor to Winchester, intending to have gone to Hampton[19] and to have viewed his navy, but hearing of the ambassadors approaching, tarried still at Winchester, where the said French lords showed themselves very honorably before the King, sitting in his throne imperial, with his lords spiritual and temporal and a great multitude of the commons there for that intent assembled. At a time prefixed, the Archbishop of Bourges made an eloquent and a long oration, dissuading war, and praising peace, offering to the King of England a great sum of money with divers base and poor countries with the Lady Katherine in marriage, so that he would dissolve his army and dismiss his soldiers which he had gathered and made ready. [The Archbishop declared]: ". . . Of truth, he [Charles VI] moved with pity as a lover of peace, to the intent that innocent blood should not be dispersed abroad, and that Christian people should not be afflicted with battle and destroyed with mortal war, hath made his whole affiance in God most puissant, according to right and reason, trusting in his quarrel to be aided and supported by his benevolent subjects and favorable well-willers. And since we be subjects and servants, we require thee to cause us safely and surely without damage to be conducted out of thy realm and dominions and that thou wilt write thine answer wholly as thou hast given it, under thy seal and sign manual." [20] [The King replied]: ". . . As concerning mine answer to be written, subscribed and sealed, I assure you that I would not speak that sentence the which I would not write and subscribe, nor subscribe that line to the which I would refuse to put my seal. Therefore your safe conduct shall be to you delivered with mine answer, and then you may depart surely and safely, I warrant you, into your country, where I trust sooner to visit you than you shall have cause to salute or bid me welcome."

Cf. also **Stow, pp. 583–88; Holinshed, pp. 1165a–72b.**

HOLINSHED, p. 1168a.

Whilst in the Lenten season (1414) the King lay at Kenilworth, there came to him from Charles, Dolphin of France, the French King's eldest son, certain ambassadors that brought with them a barrel of Paris balls, which they presented to him for a token from their master, which present was taken in very ill part, as sent in scorn, to signify that it was more meet for the King to pass the time with such childish exercise than to attempt any worthy exploit; wherefore the King wrote to him that ere long he would send to him some London balls that should break and batter down the roofs of his houses about his ears.[21]

HALL, f. HV, xi, *recto*.

When the King had ordered all things for the tuition[22] and safeguard of his realm and people, he, leaving behind him for governor of the realm the Queen, his mother-in-law,[23] departed to the town of Southampton, intending there to take ship, and so to transfreight into France.

HOLINSHED, p. 1166a.

. . . he elected the best men in the laws of the realm to the offices of justice and men of good living he preferred to high degrees and authority.[24]

Scene 11

HALL, f. HV, xii, *verso*.

When the wind was prosperous and pleasant for the navy to set forward, they weighed up the anchors and hoisted up their sails and set forward with 1500 ships on the vigil of the Assumption of our Lady and took land at Caux, commonly called Kyd Caux,[1] where the river of Seine runneth into the sea, without resistance or bloodshedding. . . . The next day after he [Henry V] marched toward the town of Harfleur standing on the river of Seine between two hills, and besieged it on every side.

HALL, f. HV, xiv, *verso*.

The French King being at Rouen, hearing that the King of England had passed the water of Somme, was not a little discontented and assembled his council to the number of thirty-five to consult what should be done. The chief whereof were the Dolphin, his son, whose name was Louis, calling himself King of Sicily,[2] [etc.]. . . . And so Mount-joy, King-at-Arms,[3] was sent to the King of England to defy him as the enemy of France, and to tell him that he should shortly have battle. King Henry soberly answered, "Sir, mine intent and desire is none other but to do as it pleaseth Almighty God and as it becometh me."

HALL, f. HV, xv, *recto*.

The Dolphin sore desired to be at that battle, but he was prohibited by the King his father.

Cf. also Stow, pp. 588–89; Holinshed, pp. 1172b–77b.

Scene 12

HALL, ff. HV, xv, *recto*–xvi, *recto*.

The King of England, informed by his spies that the day of battle was nearer than he looked for, dislodged from Bomiers and rode in good array through the fair plain beside the town of Blangy,[1] where, to the intent that his army should not be included in a strait or driven to a corner, he chose a place meet and convenient for two armies to draw up battle between the towns of Blangy and Agincourt, where he pitched his field.

The Constable of France, the Marshal, the Admiral, the Lord Rambures, Master of the Crossbows, and divers lords and knights pitched their banners near the banner royal of the Constable in the County of St. Paul within the territory of Agincourt, by the which way the Englishmen must needs pass toward Calais. The Frenchmen made great fires about their banners . . . and all that night made great cheer and were very merry. The Englishmen that night sounded their trumpets and divers musical instruments with great melody, and yet they were both hungry, weary, sore travailed and much vexed with cold diseases.

Now approached the fortunate fair day to the Englishmen and the infest[2] and unlucky day to the French nobility, which was the 25th day of October in the year of our Lord Jesus Christ 1415, being then Friday and the day of Crispin and Crispinian. . . .

[King Henry] appointed a vanguard, of which he made captain Edward Duke of York, who with a haughty courage had of the King required and obtained that office.

Cf. also Stow, pp. 593–98; Holinshed, pp. 1177b–82b.

Scene 13

HALL, f. HV, xvii.

The Frenchmen in the mean season[1] little or nothing regarding the small number of the English nation, were of such haughty courage and proud stomachs that they took no thought for the battle, as if they were victors and overcomers before any stroke was struck, and laughed at the

Englishmen, and for very pride thought themselves lifted into heaven jesting and boasting that they had the Englishmen enclosed in a strait and had overcome and taken without any resistance. The captains determined how to divide the spoil; the soldiers played [for] the Englishmen at dice; the noblemen devised a chariot how they might triumphantly convey King Henry a captive to the city of Paris. . . . I may not forget how the Frenchmen, being in this pleasant pastime, sent a herald to King Henry to inquire what ransom he would offer, and how he answered that within two or three hours he hoped that it should so happen that the Frenchmen should common[2] rather with the Englishmen how to be redeemed than the Englishmen should take thought how to pay any ransom or money for their deliverance; ascertaining[3] them for himself that his dead carrion should rather be their prey than his living body should pay any ransom.

HALL, ff. HV, xv, *verso*–xvi, *verso*.

[The oration of the Constable of France:] "Is not here the flower of the French nation on barded[4] horses with sharp spears and deadly weapons? Are not here the bold Bretons with fiery hand-guns and sharp swords? See you not present the practised men of Picardy with strong and weighty crossbows? Beside these, we have the fierce men of Brabant and strong Almains with long pikes and cutting slaughmesses.[5] And on the other side is a small handful of poor Englishmen which are entered into this region in hope of some gain or desire of profit, who by reason that their supplies are consumed and spent, they are by daily famine sore weakened, consumed, and almost without spirits. . . . For you must understand that [if] you keep an Englishman one month

from his warm bed, fat beef and stale drink, and let him at
that season taste cold and suffer hunger, you then shall see
his courage abated, his body wax lean and bare, and ever desirous to return into his own country."

SCENE 14

HALL, f. HV, xvi.

King Henry also like a leader and not like one led, like a
sovereign and not like a soldier, ordered his men for his most
advantage like an expert captain and a courageous warrior.
And first he sent privily two hundred archers into a low
meadow which was near to the forward [1] of his enemies, but
separate with a great ditch, and [they] were there commanded to keep themselves close till they had a token given
them to shoot at their adversaries. Beside this, he appointed
a vanguard, of the which he made captain Edward Duke of
York who of a haughty courage had of the King required
and obtained that office: and with him were the lords Beaumond, Willoughby and Fanhope, and this battle was all
archers. The middle guard was governed by the King himself
with his brother the Duke of Gloucester, and the Earls Marshal, Oxford and Suffolk, in which were all the strong billmen. [2] The Duke of Exeter, uncle to the King, led the rear
guard, which was mixed both with archers and billmen. The
horsemen like wings went on every side of the battle. When
the king had thus ordered his battle, like a puissant conqueror without fear of his enemies, yet considering the multitude of them far to exceed the final number of his people,
doubting that the Frenchmen would compass and beset him
about, and so fight with him on every side, to the intent to
vanquish the power of the French horsemen which might

break the order and array of his archers, in whom the whole force of the battle did consist and in manner remain, he caused stakes bound with iron sharp at both ends of the length of 5 or 6 feet, to be pitched before the archers and on every side of the footmen like an hedge, to the intent that if the barded horses ran rashly upon them, they might shortly be gored and destroyed, and appointed certain persons to remove the stakes when the archers moved, and as time required; so that the footmen were hedged about with the stakes and the horsemen stood like a bulwark between them and their enemies outside the stakes. This device of fortifying an army was at this time first invented.

Cf. also Stow, pp. 593–94; Holinshed, p. 1179a.

STOW, p. 594.

The night before this cruel battle, by the advice and counsel (as it is said) of the Duke of York, the King had given commandment through his host, that every man should purvey him a stake sharp at both ends, which the Englishmen fixed in the ground before them in the field, to defend them from the oppression of the horsemen.

HALL, f. HV, xvi, *verso*.

When he [Henry V] had ordered thus his battles, he left a small company to keep his camp and baggage, and then calling his captains and soldiers about him, he made to them an hearty oration in effect as followeth, saying: "Well beloved friends and countrymen, I exhort you heartily to think and conceive in yourselves that this day shall be to us all a day of joy, a day of good luck and a day of victory. For truly if you well note and wisely consider all things, almighty God, under whose protection we be come hither, hath ap-

pointed a place so meet and apt for our purpose as we our-
selves could neither have devised nor wished, which as it is
apt and convenient for our small number and little army so
is it unprofitable and unmeet for a great multitude to fight
or give battle in. . . . Therefore putting your only trust
in Him, let not their multitude fear [3] your hearts, nor their
great number abate your courage . . . in which good and
just quarrel all good persons shall rather set both their feet
forward than once to turn a heel backward. . . . If you
be victors and overcome your enemies, your strength and
virtue shall be spread and dispersed through the whole
world. . . . Therefore now joyously prepare yourselves to
the battle and courageously fight with your enemies, for at
this very time all the realm of England prayeth for our good
luck and prosperous success.

SCENE 15

HALL, f. HV, xx, *recto.*

Surely by the relation of the Heralds and declaration of
other notable persons worthy of credit, as Enguerrant [1]
writeth, there were slain on the French party above ten
thousand persons, whereof one hundred twenty-six were
princes and nobles bearing banners. . . . Of Englishmen at
this battle were slain Edward Duke of York, the Earl of
Suffolk, Sir Richard Chicheley and Davy Gam, Esq.,
and of all others not above twenty-five, if you will give
credit to such as write miracles. But other writers whom I
sooner believe, affirm that there was slain above five or six
hundred persons, which is not unlikely considering that the
battle was earnestly and furiously fought for the space of
three long hours. Wherefore it is not incredible nor yet im-

possible that more Englishmen than twenty-five were slain or destroyed.

HALL, ff. HV, xviii, *verso–xix, recto.*

That night he [Henry V] took refreshment of such as he found in the French camp, and in the morning Mountjoy King-at-Arms and four Heralds came to him to know the number of prisoners and to desire burial for them which were slain. . . . He demanded of them why they made to him that request, considering that he knew not certainly whether the praise and the victory were meant to be attributed to him or to their nation. "O Lord!" saith Mountjoy King-at-Arms, "think you us officers of arms to be rude and bestial persons? If we for the affection that we bear to our natural country, would either for favor or reward hide or deny your glorious victory, the fowls of the air, the worms of the ground feeding on the multitude of the dead carrions, by your sole puissance destroyed and confounded, will bear witness against us. . . ." "Well," said the King, "seeing this is your determination, I willingly accept the same, desiring you to know² the name of the castle near adjoining." When they had answered that it was called Agincourt, he said that this conflict should be called The Battle of Agincourt.

Cf. also Stow, p. 596; Holinshed, pp. 1181a–b.

SCENES 16 AND 17

HALL, f. HV, xviii, *recto.*

Certain Frenchmen on horseback, which fled first from the field at their first coming, and hearing that the English tents and pavilions were far from the army without any

great number of keepers or persons meet and convenient for
defense, partly moved and stirred with covetous desire of
spoil and prey, and partly intending by some notable act to
revenge the damage and displeasure done to them and theirs
in battle the same day, entered into the King's camp, which
was empty of men and fortified with varlets and lackeys,
and there despoiled halls, robbed tents, broke up chests and
carried away caskets and slew such servants as they could
find in the tents and pavilions. For the which act they were
long imprisoned and sore punished and like to have lost
their lives if the Dolphin had longer lived.

SCENE 18

HALL, ff. HV, xxxiii, *verso–xxxiv, recto.*

The place of the interview and meeting [in 1419] was
appointed to be beside Meulan on the river of Seine, in a
fair plain. . . . When the day of appointment approached,
the King of England . . . entered into his park and took
his lodging. Likewise for the French party thither came Isabel the French Queen because the King her husband was
fallen into his old frenetical disease . . . and she had attending on her the fair Lady Katherine her daughter and
twenty-five ladies and damsels, and had also for her furniture[1] a thousand men of war. . . . The King of England,
like a prince of great stomach and no less good behavior,
received humbly the French queen and her daughter and
them honorably embraced and familiarly kissed. . . . The
next day after, they assembled again, and the French party
brought with them the Lady Katherine, only to the intent
that the King of England, seeing and beholding so fair a lady
and so minion[2] a damsel, should so be inflamed and rapt in

love, that he to obtain so beautiful a spouse, should the sooner agree to a gentle peace and loving composition.

Cf. also Holinshed, p. 1199b.

Scene 19

HALL, f. HV, xix, *recto–verso.*

When the King of England was departed on Sunday toward Calais, divers Frenchmen repaired to the plain where the battle was and removed again the dead bodies, some to find their lords and masters and them to convey into their countries there to be buried, some to spoil and take the relics which the Englishmen had left behind. For they took nothing but gold, silver, jewels, rich apparel and costly armor. But the ploughmen and peasants spoiled the dead carcasses, leaving them neither shirt nor cloth, and so they lay stark naked till Wednesday.

. . . After the King of England had refreshed himself and his soldiers in the town of Calais . . . he with all his prisoners took shipping at Calais, and the same day landed at Dover, having with him the dead bodies of the Duke of York and the Earl of Suffolk.

HALL, f. HV, xx, *verso.*

. . . While these things were thus in working, either for melancholy that he had for the loss at Agincourt or from sudden disease, John, Dolphin of Vienois, heir apparent to Charles the French King, departed out of this natural life without issue.

Cf. also Holinshed, p. 1182b.

SCENE 20

HALL, f. HV, xxxvi, *verso*.

A tripartite truce between the two kings and the duke and their countries was determined, so that the King of England should send in the company of the Duke of Burgundy his ambassadors to Troyes in Champagne sufficiently authorized to conclude so great a matter. . . . The King, the Queen, and the Lady Katherine them received [March 21, 1420, or shortly after] and heartily welcomed, showing great signs and tokens of love and amity. After a few days they fell to council, in which it was concluded that King Henry of England should come to Troyes and marry Lady Katherine, and the King should make him heir of his realm, crown and dignity after his death and departure out of this natural life. . . . He came toward Troyes, where the Duke of Burgundy accompanied with many noble men received [him], two leagues outside the town, and conveyed him to his lodging and his princes with him, and all his army was lodged in small villages thereabouts. And after he had reposed himself, he went to visit the King, the Queen, and the Lady Katherine, whom he found in St. Peter's Church, where [there] was a joyous meeting, honorable receiving and a loving embracing on both parties, which was the 20th day of May [1420]. And there were the King and the Lady Katherine made sure together before the high altar, and on the third day of June next following they were with all solemnity espoused and married in the same church. . . . When this great matter was finished, the kings swore for their part to observe this agreement and league in all points. Likewise swore the Duke of Burgundy and a great number of princes and nobles which were present. . . . Then was he [Henry V] named and proclaimed heir and Regent of France.

Cf. also Stow, p. 605; Holinshed, pp. 1203a–4a.

NOTES TO APPENDIX A

Scene 1

1 A curious history attaches to the incipit letter used by Stow (or his printer Bynneman) to introduce this chapter on Henry of Monmouth. It evidently served to represent Prince Henry as having given his father his dagger. Professor Kenneth C. Lindsay, of Harpur College, has called my attention to the fact that the letter was, in fact, designed by Holbein the younger (d. 1543) for the English printer Wolfe. According to Sir Sidney Lee, *DNB, s.v.,* "R. Wolfe (d. 1573)," Stow "purchased some part of Wolfe's antiquarian collections" and "made much use of them in his works." The design actually illustrates the legend of Archambault (Herkinbald), Sire de Bourbon (thirteenth century), who, when on his death bed, cut his nephew's throat because the youth had violated a woman in a neighboring room; cf. Dodgson, pp. 241–43.

2 *engine:* device.

3 *other his:* his other.

4 *used:* kept.

5 (1370?–1451), court poet, disciple of Chaucer, author of *Troy Book* (begun at the request of Prince Henry), *Falls of Princes, Story of Thebes,* etc.

6 *distress:* deprive.

7 *youth:* youthfulness.

8 Stow's authority for this narrative was Titus Livius, *Vita Henrici Quinti* (after 1437), anonymously translated in 1513. Both the *Vita* and its translation are cited by Stow as early as 1570; cf. *Summary,* f. 258, *verso.* He does not, however, include this episode before 1580.

Scenes 2 and 3

1 *debate:* quarrel.

2 *put them in the King's grace:* accept the King's judgment without formal trial.

3 Stow first mentions this episode in his *Summary* (1570), f. 257, *verso*. He cites as authority the Register of Mayors.

Scene 4

1 *advertised:* notified.
2 *reserved:* except.
3 *inconvenience:* impropriety.
4 *eftsoons:* straightway.
5 *reverence:* obeisance.
6 *after:* afterwards.
7 *abrayed:* roused up.
8 *suffer semblably:* receive properly.
9 *most:* more.
10 *placability:* complaisance.
11 *unthrifty playfairs:* spendthrift playfellows.

Scenes 5 and 6

1 *act:* behavior.
2 *meanly:* moderately.
3 *advertised:* notified.
4 See Explanatory Notes: Scene 6, line 8.   Holinshed: appareled.
5 *estates:* personages.
6 *house:* attendant lords.
7 *go:* walk.
8 *redoubted:* redoubtable.
9 *my conversation:* what I have said.
10 *desirous:* desirable.
11 i.e., slaying me.
12 *for no:* despite any.
13 i.e., the defeat of the Percys and the other rebels.
14 *then:* in that case.
15 *enterprise:* undertake.

Scene 8

1 *cure:* care.
2 *advertised:* notified.
3 *misused himself:* misbehaved.
4 *not as yours:* not as being something which belonged to you.
5 *garland:* crown.

Scene 9

1 *inhibiting:* commanding.
2 *by:* by his relationship to.

3 Although Henry's first embassies were concerned with the internal affairs of France, not with establishing his claim to the French throne, he soon discerned that the time was ripe to make such a claim.

4 *intreat of:* discuss.

5 *preferred:* promoted. Thomas Arundel, who had crowned Henry V, died February 20, 1414; cf. Stow, p. 585.

6 *wilful:* voluntary.

7 *divoluted:* come down.

8 (1292–1358).

9 (1268–1314).

10 Num. 27 : 8: "If a man die, and have no son, then ye shall cause his inheritance to pass unto his daughter."

11 *the Gallican descent:* the royal lineage of France. An attempt was made at this time to apply the Salic law in France. Cf. *Henry V*, I, 2, 38–41:

> "In terram Salicam mulieres ne succedant"—
> "No woman shall succeed in Salic land."
> Which Salic land the French unjustly gloze
> To be the realm of France.

12 *conditions:* characters.

13 i.e., those who are urging the prior invasion of Scotland.

14 Charles VI (1380–1422).

15 Katherine of Valois (1401–1437).

16 *age:* life.

17 *experimented:* tested.

18 They were newly arrived from France.

19 Southampton.

20 *sign manual:* signature.

21 This passage, omitted in the 1587 edition of Holinshed, was certainly used by the playwright of *The Famous Victories;* cf. Scene 9, lines 119 ff.

22 *tuition:* protection.

23 Joan of Navarre (1370?–1437); more accurately, stepmother of Henry V. She was later suspected of treason and replaced in this office by the Duke of Bedford; cf. Holinshed, pp. 1168b, 1198a.

24 This passage may have suggested the promotion of the Chief Justice to be Protector of the Realm (Scene 9, line 168), instead of the Queen Mother, as above.

Scene 11

1 See Explanatory Notes: Scene 11, line 24.

2 d. 1415.

3 Chief heraldic officer.

Scene 12

1 Blangy-sur-Ternoise, 3½ miles S.E. of Agincourt.
2 *infest:* hateful.

Scene 13

1 *mean season:* meanwhile.
2 *common:* confer together.
3 *ascertaining:* informing.
4 equipped with leather armor.
5 *slaughmesses:* ?

Scene 14

1 *forward:* front ranks.
2 *billmen:* halberdiers.
3 *fear:* terrify.

Scene 15

1 Enguerrand de Monstrelet (*c.* 1400–1453), French chronicler.
2 *desiring you to know:* requesting you that I should know.

Scene 18

1 *furniture:* attendance.
2 *minion:* delicate.

APPENDIX B

The Marginal Annotations in a Copy of Hall

Of considerable interest in the present argument is the now familiar thesis of Alan Keen and Roger Lubbock[1] that the marginal annotations (406 in number) in their copy of the 1550 edition of Edward Hall's *The Union of the Two Noble and Illustrious Families of Lancaster and York* are in the youthful hand of William Shakespeare. Hall, we have seen, was a principal source for the anonymous playwright of *The Famous Victories*. If I am right in my belief that Shakespeare wrote that play, and if Keen and Lubbock are right that the marginal annotations, in Shakespeare's hand, date from early in the 1580's, we might expect to find a significant correlation between the notations and the play.

The annotations begin, where Hall's account and Shakespeare's *Richard II* begin, with the quarrel between Hereford and Norfolk over the murder of Gloucester. They continue steadily through the reigns of Henry IV and Henry V, ending early in the reign of Henry VI. Thus they

---

[1] In their book *The Annotator* (1954), *passim*.

cover the events of four of the plays, and about half of them
are apropos of the materials dramatized. As for the hand-
writing, Keen and Lubbock maintain that while the evidence does not establish the case beyond question, it is
probable that "Shakespeare and the Annotator were the
same man." [2] I cannot accept as convincing the attempt to
follow Shakespeare's activities in Lancashire; this is no neces-
sary part of the argument as to the authorship of the annotations, since it is based solely on the identification of a
signature found in the book. I am of the opinion that the
character of the annotations itself warrants the principal
thesis. As its authors have shown, there are many striking
similarities in point of view and language between the annotations and the canonical texts.[3]

---

[2] *Op. cit.*, p. 163.

[3] To offer an example not cited by Keen and Lubbock, deriving from
Hall, f. HV, xxix, *verso:* "The goddess of war called Bellona . . . hath iii
handmaids ever of necessity attending on her, blood, fire, and famine,
which three damosels be of that force and strength that every one of them
alone is able and sufficient to torment and afflict a proud prince." The
Annotator commented: "Bellona, Goddess of Battle, hath iii handmaids:
blood, fire, and famine." The following passages from the plays may be
instanced:

(1) *Talbot.* You tempt the fury of my *three attend*ants—
     Lean *famine*, quartering steel, and climbing *fire—*
                                          (*1 Henry VI*, iv, 2, 10–11)

(2) *Chorus.* . . . at his [Henry V's] heels,
     *Lea*shed in like hounds, should *famine*, sword and *fire*
     Crouch for employment. . . .
                                          (*Henry V*, Prologue, 6–8)

(3) *Hotspur.* They come like sacrifices in their trim,
     And to the *fire*-eyed *maid* of smoky war [Bellona]
     All hot and *bleeding* will we offer them.

     The mailèd Mars shall on his altar sit
     Up to the ears in *blood*. I am on fire.
                                          (*1 Henry IV*, iv, 1, 113–17)

(4) *Ross.* . . . Bellona's bridegroom [Macbeth]
                                          (*Macbeth*, i, 2, 54)

I present herewith a series of parallel passages, on the basis of which significant comparisons between the Annotator and the anonymous dramatist can be established:

I.   Hall, f. HV, i, *recto* [4]

For imprisonment of one of his wanton mates and unthrifty play-fairs he struck the Chief Justice with his fist on the face.

Annotator

King Henry, being but Prince, struck the Chief Justice on the face for imprisoning of a wanton companion of his

The Famous Victories, Scene 4

2 Henry IV, I, 2, 217–19

FALSTAFF [*to the* CHIEF JUSTICE]. . . . For the box of the ear that the Prince gave you, he gave it like a rude prince, and you took it like a sensible lord. . . .

Comment: The Annotator omits "with his fist," and the playwright and Shakespeare prefer "a box on the ear."

II.   Hall, f. HIV, xxxii, *verso*

"Well, fair son," said the King with a great sigh, "what right I had to it [the crown] and how I enjoyed it God knoweth!" . . . short-

---

[4] Readers who wish to check Keen and Lubbock against Hall will observe that their citations from the chronicle are not based on the usual system of folio reference. I have here changed these to conform with the usage employed throughout this book.

ly after [he] departed to God, in a chamber of the Abbot of West-minster called Jerusalem the 20th day of March in the year of our Lord 1413 and in the year of his age 46, when he had reigned thir-teen years, five months and odd days in much perplexity and little pleasure. . . ."

Annotator

King Henry seemeth to confess that he had the crown wrongfully and died Anno Domini 1413. He reigned xiii years and v months. . . .

The Famous Victories, 8, 64–65

KING [HENRY]. . . . God knows, my son, how hardly I came by it [the crown], and how hardly I have maintained it.

2 Henry IV, IV, 5, 184–87

KING HENRY. . . . God knows, my son,
By what bypaths and indirect crooked ways
I met this crown, and I myself know well
How troublesome it sat upon my head.

Comment: The Annotator, the anonymous playwright, and Shakespeare note in Hall the King's compunctions about the legitimacy and difficulties of his reign.

———

III.   Hall, f. HV, i, *recto*

[King Henry] elected and chose men of gravity, men of wit, and men of high policy.

Annotator

Sage counsellors chosen

The Famous Victories, 9, 167 ff.

2 Henry IV, v, 2, 118–37

KING HENRY [*to the* CHIEF JUSTICE]. You shall be as
  father to my youth.
My voice shall sound as you do prompt mine ear . . .
And let us choose such limbs of noble counsel
That the great body of our state may go
In equal rank with the best governed nation . . .

Comment: The Annotator, the anonymous playwright, and
Shakespeare remark the same passage. Cf. Item XIII, below.

———

IV.   Hall, f. HV, i, *recto*

[King Henry] banished and separated from him all his old flatterers
and familiar companions (not unrewarded nor yet unpreferred)
inhibiting them upon a great pain not once to approach either to his
speech or presence, nor yet to lodge or sojourn within ten miles of
his court or mansion.

Annotator

All flatterers and old companions banished x mile from the court

The Famous Victories, 9, 45–56

KING [HENRY]. . . . my unfeigned grief is not to be ruled by
thy flattering and dissembling talk. . . . Ah, Tom, your former life
grieves me, and makes me to abandon and abolish your company
forever. And therefore, not upon pain of death to approach my
presence by ten miles space. Then, if I hear well of you, it may be
I will do somewhat for you. . . .

2 Henry IV, v, 5, 67–71

KING HENRY [*to* FALSTAFF]. Till then, I banish thee, on
    pain of death,
As I have done the rest of my misleaders,
Not to come near our person by ten mile.
For competence of life I will allow you,
That lack of means enforce you not to evil.

Comment: The Annotator and Shakespeare say "ten mile";
Hall and the anonymous playwright have "ten miles."

V.   Hall, f. HV, ii, *verso*

During this first year, Sir John Oldcastle, which by his wife was
called Lord Cobham, a valiant captain and an hardy gentleman, was
accused to the Archbishop of Canterbury of certain points of heresy.

Annotator

. . . Sir John Oldcastle Lord Cobham condemned for heresy

Comment: The Annotator points out an ancestor of the
Cobhams.

VI.   Hall, f. HV, v, *recto*

[The Archbishop of Canterbury finds Henry V] "very heir to
Queen Isabel, your great grandmother, daughter to King Philip the
Fair and sister and heir to three kings who died without issue."

Annotator

Queen Isabel, daughter to King Philip, heir to three Kings dying
without issue, by whom King Henry claimed

The Famous Victories, 9, 62–63

. . . your great grandmother Isabel, wife to King Edward the Third, and sister to Charles, the French King.

Henry V, I, 2, 81

. . . fair Queen Isabel, his grandmother

———

VII. Hall, f. HV, vii, *verso*

. . . the old, ancient proverb . . . which sayeth, "He that will France win, must with Scotland first begin."

Annotator

He that will France win with Scotland he must begin

Holinshed (1577), II, 1169b

"Whoso will France win, must with Scotland first begin."

[This is reported as an "old saying."]

The Famous Victories, 9, 71–73

. . . I think it therefore best to conquer Scotland; and then I think that you may go more easily into France.

Henry V, I, 2, 167–68

"If that you will France win,
Then with Scotland first begin."

[This is reported as "a saying very old and true."]

.   .   .

Hall, f. HV, vii, *verso*

"He that will Scotland win, let him with France first begin."

Annotator

He that will Scotland win, let him with France first begin

Holinshed (1577), II, 1169b

". . . he which would Scotland win with France must begin."

The Famous Victories, 9, 78–80

"He that will Scotland win must first with France begin," according to the old saying.

Comment: Here chief interest attaches to the sequence of phrases: *the old, ancient proverb which sayeth; an old saying; a saying very old and true; the old saying.* Hall and Holinshed are read by the anonymous playwright and Shakespeare.

VIII.   Hall, f. HV, ix, *recto*

The English ambassadors according to their commission required of the French King to deliver to the King of England the realm and crown of France.

Annotator

The commission to require the crown of France, etc.

The Famous Victories, 9, 28–30

. . . he sent his embassage into France to tell the French King that Harry of England hath sent for the crown . . .

IX. Hall, f. HV, ix, *verso*

[The Dolphin] sent to King Henry a tun of tennis balls to play with.

Annotator

A tun of tennis balls sent as is reported

Holinshed (1577), II, 1168a

. . . a barrel of Paris balls.

The Famous Victories, 9, 119–22

KING. What, a guilded tun! I pray you, my Lord of York, look what is in it.

YORK. If it please your Grace, here is a carpet, and a tun of tennis balls.

Henry V, I, 2, 254–58

FIRST AMBASSADOR. He therefore sends you, meeter for your spirit,
This tun of treasure, and, in lieu of this,
Desires you let the dukedoms that you claim
Hear no more of you. This the Dauphin speaks.
KING HENRY. What treasure, Uncle?
EXETER. Tennis balls, my liege.

Comment: The anonymous playwright is closer to Hall and the Annotator than to Holinshed; he adds the item that the tun was "guilded." Shakespeare, whose "tun of treasure" was also doubtless guilded, takes his phrasing from Hall **via** *The Famous Victories* and, perhaps, the Annotator.

X.   Hall, f. HV, x, *recto*

[The Archbishop of Bourges speaks], praising peace and offering to the King of England a great sum of money with divers base and poor countries with the Lady Katherine in marriage. . . .

Annotator

An offer of Lady Katherine and other base countries for peace

The Famous Victories, 9, 106–9

[The Archbishop reports that the French King], not minding to shed innocent blood, is rather content to yield somewhat to your [King Henry's] unreasonable demands—that, if fifty thousand crowns a year, with his daughter, the said Lady Katherine, in marriage . . .

Henry V, iii, *Prologue,* 28–31

Chorus. . . . Suppose the Ambassador from the French comes back,
Tells Harry that the King doth offer him
Katherine his daughter, and with her, to dowry,
Some petty and unprofitable dukedoms.

———

XI.   Hall, f. HV, x, *verso*

[Bourges speaks to King Henry]: ". . . We require thee to cause us safely and surely without damage to be conducted out of thy realm and dominions and that thou wilt write thine answer wholly as thou hast given it, under thy seal and sign manual."

Annotator

A stout bishop of France so in defiance of a prince to speak

The Famous Victories, 9, 141–42

ARCHBISHOP. I beseech your Grace to deliver me your safe conduct under your broad seal emanuel. [Cf. Explanatory Note on Scene 9, line 142.]

Henry V, I, 2, 297

KING HENRY. . . . Convey them with safe conduct.

———

XII. Hall, f. HV, x, *verso*

[King Henry speaks]: "Concerning mine answer to be written, subscribed, and sealed, I assure you that I would not speak that sentence which I would not write and subscribe, nor subscribe that line to the which I would refuse to put my seal. . . ."

Annotator

The answer of the King of England

The Famous Victories, 9, 143–45

KING [HENRY]. Priest of Bourges, know that the hand and seal of a king . . . is all one. And, instead of my hand and seal I will bring him [the French king] my hand and sword.

———

XIII. Hall, f. HV, xi, *recto*

. . . for the tuition and safeguard of his realm and people, he, leaving behind him for governor of the realm the Queen, his mother-in-law . . .

Annotator

The King's mother-in-law governor of the said realm in his absence

The Famous Victories, 9, 167–68

KING [HENRY]. . . . . I have chosen you [the Chief Justice] to be my Protector over my realm . . .

Comment: The playwright allows himself a poet's license; cf. pp. 99–100, and above, Item III.

————

XIV.   Hall, f. HV, xiv, *verso*

And so Mountjoy, King-at-Arms, was sent to the King of England to defy him as the enemy of France.

Annotator

Mountjoy, King-at-Arms, sent in defiance to King Henry

The Famous Victories, 12, 20–24

KING [HENRY]. . . . . How now, what is that?
YORK. I think it be some herald of arms.
                    Enter a HERALD.
HERALD. King of England, my Lord High Constable and others of the noblemen of France send me to defy thee as open enemy to God, our country, and us . . .

Henry V, III, 6, 121–24

[*Tucket. Enter* MONTJOY.]
MONTJOY. You know me by my habit.
KING HENRY. Well then, I know thee. What shall I know of thee?
MONTJOY. My master's mind.
KING HENRY. Unfold it.

XV.   Hall, f. HV, xv, *verso*

. . . surely they were esteemed to be in number six times as many or
more than was the whole company of the Englishmen.

Annotator

Great odds between the English army and the French

The Famous Victories, 14, 9–10

They are a hundred thousand, and we fourteen thousand! Ten to
one!

Henry V, IV, 3, 3–5

WESTMORELAND. Of fighting men they have full threescore thou-
sand.
   EXETER. There's five to one. Besides, they are all fresh.
   SALISBURY. God's arm strike with us! 'Tis a fearful odds.

Comment: Similar repercussions in Hall's readers.

XVI.   Hall, f. HV, xv, *verso*

[The oration of the Constable of France]: ". . . And on the other
side is a small handful of poor Englishmen which are entered into
this region in hope of some gain or desire of profit, who by reason
that their supplies are consumed and spent, they are by daily famine
sore weakened, consumed, and almost without spirits. . . . For you
must understand that [if] you keep an Englishman one month from
his warm bed, fat beef, and stale drink, and let him at that season
taste cold and suffer hunger, you then shall see his courage abated,
his body wax lean and bare, and ever desirous to return into his own
country."

Annotator

The French man noteth the nature of the English man

An oration of their Captain against the English army much coura-geous, first affirming the English army weak . . .

The Famous Victories, 13, 39–51

CAPTAIN. I am glad, and yet with a kind of pity, to see the poor King . . . a site of poor English scabs! Why, take an English-man out of his warm bed and his stale drink but one month, and, alas! what will become of him?

Comment: The identity of the Annotator and the anony-mous playwright is strongly suggested by their agreement in calling the speaker a Captain. In *Henry V*, III, 7, 145–65, his sentiments about the English are expressed by the Con-stable of France (as in Hall), Lord Rambures, and the Duke of Orleans.

––––––

XVII.   Hall, f. HV, xvi

King Henry also like a leader and not like one led, like a sovereign and not like a soldier, ordered his men for his most advantage like an expert captain and a courageous warrior. . . . When the King had thus ordered his battle, like a puissant conqueror without fear of his enemies, yet considering the multitude of them far to exceed the final number of his people, doubting that the Frenchmen would com-pass and beset him about, and so fight with him on every side, . . . he caused stakes bound with iron sharp at both ends . . . to be pitched before the archers and on every side of the footmen like an hedge . . .

Annotator

A notable order of King Henry his battle

The inventing of stakes which now I think be morris pikes

The Famous Victories, 14, 14–28

KING [HENRY]. Now, my lords, I will that my uncle, the Duke of York [etc.]. . . . Then I will that every archer provide him a stake of a tree, and sharpen it at both ends; and, at the first encounter of the horsemen, to pitch their stakes down into the ground before them, that they may gore themselves upon them; . . .

1 Henry VI, I, 1, 116–18

He [Talbot] wanted pikes to set before his archers,
Instead whereof sharp stakes plucked out of hedges
They pitched in the ground confusedly. . . .

Richard III, v, 3, 292–300

KING RICHARD. . . . Thus my battle shall be ordered:
My foreward shall be drawn out all in length,
Consisting equally of horse and foot,
Our archers shall be placèd in the midst.
John Duke of Norfolk, Thomas Earl of Surrey,
Shall have the leading of this foot and horse.
They thus directed, we will follow
In the main battle, whose puissance on either side
Shall be well wingèd with our chiefest horse.

Comment: The Annotator, the playwright of *The Famous Victories*, and Shakespeare agree in their interest in the passage from Hall cited above. The playwright inserted new topical references in his version of the King's ordering of the battle and paraphrased Hall's description of the device of the stakes. In *1 Henry VI*, Shakespeare copied both Hall and the playwright in the matter of the stakes. In *Richard III*, he imitated the ordering of the battle. See pp. 125–26; 183–92.

XVIII.   Hall, f. HV, xvi, *verso*

[The King speaks to his soldiers]: ". . . Therefore now joyously prepare yourselves to the battle and courageously fight with your enemies, for at this very time all the realm of England prayeth for our good luck and prosperous success. . . ."

Annotator

At the end of King Henry his oration he concludeth that England prayeth for their success

The Famous Victories, 14, 55–56

KING [HENRY]. Then is it good time, no doubt, for all England prayeth for us.

Comment: A point of interest both to the Annotator and to the author of *The Famous Victories.*

XIX.   Hall, f. HV, xvii, *verso*

. . . messengers were sent the cities and towns adjoining, willing them to make open plays and triumphs (as though that the victory were to them certain and no resistance could appear) . . .

Annotator

A triumph of the Frenchmen before victory

The Famous Victories, 14, 35–36

KING [HENRY]. Well, my lords, our battles are ordained, and the French making of bonfires, and at their banquets.

Henry V, IV, *Prologue*, 17–19

CHORUS. Proud of their numbers and secure in soul,
The confident and overlusty French
Do the low-rated English play at dice . . .

XX.   Hall, f. HV, xviii, *recto*

Certain Frenchmen on horseback, to the number of vi c horsemen,
which fled first from the field at their first coming, and hearing that
the English tents and pavilions were far from the army. . . there
despoiled halls, robbed tents, [etc.].

Annotator

A cowardly act of vi c horsemen of France

The Famous Victories, 16, 10–11

. . . the King's tents are set afire, and all they that speak English will
be killed.

Henry V, IV, 7, 7–8

. . . they have burned and carried away all that was in the King's
tent . . .

XXI.   Hall, f. HV, xix, *recto*

[King Henry asked] to know the name of the castle near adjoining.
When they had answered that it was called Agincourt, he said that
this conflict should be called The Battle of Agincourt.

Annotator

The castle of Agincourt gave name to the battle

The Famous Victories, 15, 35–41

KING [HENRY]. . . . what castle is this so near adjoining to our camp?

HERALD. If it please your Majesty, 'tis called the Castle of Agincourt.

KING [HENRY]. Well, then, my lords of England, for the more honor of our Englishmen, I will that this be forever called The Battle of Agincourt.

Henry V, IV, 7, 91–93

KING HENRY. . . . What is this castle called that stands hard by?

MONTJOY. They call it Agincourt.

KING HENRY. Then call we this the field of Agincourt . . .

XXII.   Hall, f. HV, xx, *recto*

. . . there were slain on the French party above ten thousand persons, whereof were princes and nobles bearing banners cxxvi, and all the remnant saving xvi c were knights, esquires, and gentlemen. . . . Of Englishmen at this battle were slain Edward duke of York, the earl of Suffolk, Sir Richard Kikely, and Davy Gam, Esq., and of all other not above xxv, if you will give credit to such as write miracles. But other writers, whom I sooner believe, affirm that there was slain above v or vi c persons, which is not unlike . . .

Annotator

A marvelous number of dukes, earls, lords and knights of the French Army slain

Some write that only xxv Englishmen were slain but some other say that v or vi c were slain

The Famous Victories, 15, 5–10

OXFORD. . . . there are of the French army slain above ten thousand twenty-six hundred, whereof are princes and nobles bearing banners; besides, all the nobility of France are taken prisoners. Of your Majesty's army are slain none but the good Duke of York, and not above five or six and twenty common soldiers.

Henry V, IV, 8, 85–111

KING HENRY. This note doth tell me of ten thousand French
That in the field lie slain. Of Princes in this number,
And nobles bearing banners, there lie dead
One hundred twenty-six. Added to these . . .
The rest are Princes, barons, lords, knights, squires . . .
Where is the number of our English dead?
Edward the Duke of York, the Earl of Suffolk,
Sir Richard Ketly, Davy Gam, esquire.
None else of name, and of all other men
But five and twenty.

Comment: Whereas the Annotator, reporting the larger estimate of the English losses, says that "some other say that v or vi c were slain," the anonymous playwright has "five or six and twenty." The repeated "five or six" seems significant.

XXIII. Hall, f. HV, xxxvi, *verso*

. . . it was concluded that King Henry of England should come to Troyes and marry Lady Katherine, and the King should make him heir of his realm . . . and on the third of June next following they were with all solemnity espoused and married in the same church.

Annotator

A peace with condition that our King should marry the Lady Katherine, daughter of the French King, and be heir of France after him

King Henry and Lady Katherine married the 3 of June

The Famous Victories, Scenes 18 and 20

Summary Comment

These analogues serve several purposes in this argument and, accordingly, may be grouped in various ways:

(1) A few serve simply to show that the anonymous playwright and the Annotator shared an interest in Hall: Items v, vi, viii, xii, xiii, xx, xxiii.

(2) Others more cogently suggest that the anonymous playwright and the Annotator were identical: Items i, ii, iii, ix, xvii, xviii, xix, xxi.

(3) Two are so close in point of phrasing that no other conclusion seems warranted than that the anonymous playwright and the Annotator were identical: Items xvi and xxii.

(4) Several of the analogues suggest the identity of Shakespeare and the anonymous playwright as the author of the annotations: Items i, ii, iii, xv, xxi.

(5) Two offer almost conclusive proof of the identity of Shakespeare and the anonymous playwright as author of the annotations: Items ix, xvii.

(6) Two, while proving nothing about the authorship of the annotations, argue for the identity of Shakespeare and the anonymous playwright: Items vii, xi.

(7) Three analogues, on linguistic grounds, argue with special force that Shakespeare wrote the annotations: Items iv, x, xiv.

APPENDIX C

Books and Articles Used

Adams, J. Q., ed., *The Famous Victories of Henry the Fifth*, in *Chief Pre-Shakespearean Dramas*, Boston, Houghton Mifflin, 1924.
——, *A Life of Shakespeare*, Boston, Houghton Mifflin, 1923.
Ames, J., and Herbert, W., *Typographical Antiquities*, London, 1785–90.
Archbold, W. A. J., "Charles Neville (1543–1601)," *Dict. Nat. Biog.*
Bartlett, J., *A New and Complete Concordance to Words in Shakespeare*, London and New York, Macmillan, 1894.
Black, J. B., *The Reign of Elizabeth*, Oxford, Clarendon, 1936.
Bradbrook, M. C., *Shakespeare and Elizabethan Poetry*, London, Chatto and Windus, 1951.
Brooke, C. F. T., ed., *Shakespeare Apocrypha*, Oxford, Clarendon, 1918.
Burke, J. B., *A Genealogical and Heraldic Dictionary of the Peerage*, London, Harrison, 1883.
Butler, Pierce, *Materials for the Life of Shakespeare*, Chapel Hill, University of North Carolina Press, 1930.
Camden, W., *Annals*, London, Fisher, 1625. (State University of Iowa Library.)
Chambers, E. K., *The Elizabethan Stage*, Oxford, Clarendon, 1923.
——, *William Shakespeare*, Oxford, Clarendon, 1930.

Chambers, R. W., *Man's Unconquerable Mind*, Philadelphia, Saifer, 1953.

Cheyney, E. P., *Readings in English History*, New York, Ginn, 1922.

The Chronicle History of King Leir, in *Shakespeare's Library*, ed. by W. C. Hazlitt, vol. 6, London, Reeves and Turner, 1875.

Churchill, G. B., *Richard the Third up to Shakespeare*, Berlin, Mayer and Müller, 1900.

Coleridge, S. T., *Literary Criticism*, ed. by J. W. Mackail, Oxford, Clarendon, 1921.

Craig, H., ed., *William Shakespeare*, complete works, Chicago, Scott, Foresman, 1951.

Daniel, P. A., Intro. to *The Famous Victories of Henry the Fifth*, Quarto of 1598, facsimile in photolithography, London, Praetorius, 1887.

Daniel, S., *Complete Works*, ed. by A. B. Grosart, London, Hazell, Watson, and Viney, 1885–96.

Dodgson, C., "An Illustration by Holbein of the Legend of Herkinbald," *Journal of the Warburg and Courtauld Institutes*, III (1940), 241–43.

Elyot, T., *The Book Named the Governor* (Everyman's Library), London, Dent, 1907.

Evans, G. B., "Supplement to *Henry IV*, *Part I*, New Variorum Edition," in *Shakespeare Quarterly*, VII (Summer, 1956).

Everitt, E. B., *The Young Shakespeare*, Copenhagen, Rosenkilde and Bagger, 1954.

The Famous Victories of Henry the Fifth: Containing the Honorable Battle of Agin-Court: As It Was Played by the Queen's Majesty's Players. London: Printed by Thomas Creed, *1598*. (Facsimile in photolithography, London, Praetorius, 1887.)

The Famous Victories of Henry the Fifth: Containing the Honorable Battle of Agin-Court: As It Was Acted by the King's Majesty's Servants. London: Printed by Bernard Alsop. *1617*. (Folger Shakespeare Library.)

The Famous Victories of Henry the Fifth, Quarto of 1617, in J. Nichols, *Six Old Plays*, London, Leacroft, 1779.

The Famous Victories of Henry the Fifth, Quarto of 1617, ed. by A. F. Hopkinson, London, Sims, 1896.

The Famous Victories of Henry the Fifth, in *Chief Pre-Shakespearean Dramas*, ed. by J. Q. Adams, Boston, Houghton Mifflin, 1924.

Field, B., ed., *The True Tragedy of Richard III*, London, Shakespeare Society, 1844.

The First English Life of King Henry the Fifth, ed. by C. L. Kingsford, Oxford, Clarendon, 1911.

The First Part of the Contention betwixt York and Lancaster, in *The First Sketches of the Second and Third Parts of King Henry the Sixth*, ed. by J. O. Halliwell-Phillips, London, Shakespeare Society, 1843.

Fleay, F. G., *A Biographical Chronicle of the English Drama, 1559–1642*, London, Reeves and Turner, 1891.

Froude, J. A., *History of England from the Fall of Wolsey to the Defeat of the Spanish Armada*, London, Longmans, Green, 1870–75.

Goddard, H. C., *The Meaning of Shakespeare*, Chicago, University of Chicago Press, 1951.

Greer, C. A., "A Lost Play the Source of Shakespeare's *Henry IV* and *Henry V*," *Notes and Queries*, n.s. 1, February, 1954.

———, "Shakespeare's Use of *The Famous Victories of Henry the Fifth*," *Notes and Queries*, n.s. 1, June, 1954.

Greg, W. W., ed., *Henslowe's Diary*, London, Bullen, 1904–08.

———, *Two Elizabethan Stage Abridgements*, Oxford, Clarendon, 1923.

Hall, Edward, *The Union of the Two Noble and Illustrious Families of Lancaster and York*, London, Grafton, 1550.

Halliday, F. E., *A Shakespeare Companion*, London, Duckworth, 1952.

Halliwell-Phillips, J. O., ed., *The First Part of the Contention betwixt York and Lancaster*, in *The First Sketches of the Second and Third Parts of King Henry the Sixth*, London, Shakespeare Society, 1843.

———, *Outlines of the Life of Shakespeare*, London, Longmans, Green, 1887.

———, *Poetical Miscellanies*, London, Percy Society, 1845.

———, ed., *Tarlton's Jests*, London, Shakespeare Society, 1844.

Harrison, G. B., ed., *Shakespeare: The Complete Works*, New York, Harcourt, Brace, 1952.

Harvey, G., *Four Letters and Certain Sonnets, 1592.* London, Lane, 1922.

Hemingway, S. B., ed., *Henry the Fourth, Part I*, New Variorum, Philadelphia and London, Lippincott, 1936.

Henderson, T. F., "Henry Hastings (1535–1595)," *Dict. Nat. Biog.*

Henslowe, P., *Diary*, ed. by W. W. Greg, London, Bullen, 1904–08.

Herbert, W., *see* Ames.

Hoffman, C., *The Murder of the Man Who Was 'Shakespeare,'* New York, Messner, 1955.

Holinshed, R., *The Chronicles of England, Scotland, and Ireland,* London, Harrison, 1577. (Folger Shakespeare Library.)

———, *The Chronicles of England, Scotland, and Ireland,* London, Harrison, 1587. (Folger Shakespeare Library.)

Hopkinson, F. A., ed., *The Famous Victories of Henry the Fifth,* Quarto of 1617, London, Sims, 1896.

Johnson, S., *Preface to Shakespeare, 1765,* in Smith, D. N., *Shakespeare Criticism,* London, Milford, 1926.

Keats, J., *Letters,* ed. by M. B. Forman, London, Milford, 1935.

Keen, A., and Lubbock, R., *The Annotator,* New York, Macmillan, 1954.

Kingsford, C. L., ed., *The First English Life of King Henry the Fifth,* Oxford, Clarendon, 1911. A translation from the Latin of Titus Livius, *Vita Henrici Quinti* (after 1437).

———, ed., Stow, J., *A Survey of London, 1603,* Oxford, Clarendon, 1908.

Kittredge, G. L., ed., Shakespeare, W., *Hamlet,* Boston, Ginn, 1939.

Knights, L. C., *Explorations,* London, Chatto and Windus, 1946.

Lee, S., "Peregrine Bertie (1555–1601)," *Dict. Nat. Biog.*

———, "Henry Percy (1532?–1585)," *Dict. Nat. Biog.*

———, "Henry Percy (1564–1632)," *Dict. Nat. Biog.*

———, "John Stow (1525?–1605)," *Dict. Nat. Biog.*

———, "Richard Tarlton (d. 1588)," *Dict. Nat. Biog.*

———, "R. Wolfe (d. 1573)," *Dict. Nat. Biog.*

Livius, Titus, *see* Kingsford (1911).

Lubbock, R., *see* Keen.

Malone, E., ed., *The Plays and Poems of William Shakespeare,* London, Rivington, 1821.

Maxwell, B., *Studies in the Shakespeare Apocrypha,* New York, Columbia University Press, 1956.

Michel, L., and Seronsy, C., "Shakespeare's History Plays and Daniel," *Studies in Philology,* LII (October, 1955).

Monaghan, J., "Falstaff's Forbears," *Studies in Philology,* XVIII (July, 1921).

Morgan, A. E., *Some Problems of Shakespeare's Henry the Fourth,* London, Milford, 1924.

Nash, T., *Complete Works,* ed. by R. B. McKerrow, London, Bullen, 1904–10.

Nichols, J., *The Progresses and Public Processions of Queen Elizabeth,* London, 1823.

Ogburn, D. and C., *This Star of England,* Coward-McCann, 1952.

Pitcher, S. M., "Alas, poor Yorick!" *Philological Quarterly,* XXI (April, 1942).

Pollard, A., "Henry Stanley (1531–1593)," *Dict. Nat. Biog.*

———, and Wilson, J. D., "The 'Stolne and Surreptitious' Shakespearean Texts," *London Times Literary Supplement*, January 9, March 13, 1919.

The Roxburghe Ballads, ed. by W. Chappell and J. W. Ebsworth, Hertford, Austin, 1871–99.

Rymer, T., *Critical Works*, ed. by C. A. Zimansky, New Haven, Yale University Press, 1956.

Seronsy, C., *see* Michel.

Shaaber, M. A., ed., *Henry the Fourth, Part II*, New Variorum, Philadelphia and London, Lippincott, 1940.

Sir John Oldcastle, in *Shakespeare Apocrypha*, ed. by C. F. T. Brooke, Oxford, Clarendon, 1918.

Smart, J., *Shakespeare Truth and Tradition*, London, Arnold, 1928.

Solly-Flood, F., "The Story of Prince Henry of Monmouth and Chief-Justice Gascoign," London, *Transactions of the Royal Historical Society*, n.s. 4, 1886.

Stoll, E. E., "Falstaff," *Modern Philology*, XII (October, 1914).

Stow, J., *The Annals of England*, London, 1590, 1592, 1601, 1605. (Folger Shakespeare Library.)

———, *The Chronicles of England*, London, 1580. (Folger Shakespeare Library.)

———, *Summary of English Chronicles*, London, 1565, 1566, 1570, 1573, 1579, 1598, 1604. (Folger Shakespeare Library.)

———, *A Survey of London, 1603*, ed. by C. L. Kingsford, Oxford, Clarendon, 1908.

Sykes, H. D., *The Authorship of The Taming of the Shrew, The Famous Victories of Henry V, and the Additions to Marlowe's Faustus*, London, Chatto and Windus, 1920.

Symonds, J. A., *Shakespeare's Predecessors*, London, Smith, Elder, 1884.

Tarlton's Jests, ed. by J. O. Halliwell-Phillips, London, Shakespeare Society, 1844.

Tilley, M. P., *A Dictionary of Proverbs in England in the Sixteenth and Seventeenth Centuries*, Ann Arbor, University of Michigan Press, 1950.

Tillyard, E. M. W., *Shakespeare's History Plays*, London, Chatto and Windus, 1944.

Traversi, D. A., *Shakespeare from Richard II to Henry V*, Stanford, Stanford University Press, 1957.

The True Tragedy of Richard III, ed. by B. Field, London, Shakespeare Society, 1844.

Ward, B. M., *"The Famous Victories of Henry the Fifth:* Its Place in Elizabethan Dramatic Literature," *Review of English Studies,* IV (July, 1928).

————, *The Seventeenth Earl of Oxford (1550–1642),* London, Murray, 1928.

Wilson, F. P., *Marlowe and the Early Shakespeare,* Oxford, Clarendon, 1953.

Wilson, J. D., ed., Shakespeare, W., *The First Part of Henry IV,* Cambridge, Cambridge University Press, 1946.

————, *The Fortunes of Falstaff,* New York, Macmillan, 1944.

————, *Life in Shakespeare's England,* Cambridge, Cambridge University Press, 1911.

————, "The Origins and Development of Shakespeare's *Henry IV,*" *The Library,* ser. 4, vol. 26 (June, 1945).

————, *see also* Pollard.